The Q Guide to

NYC Pride

The Q Guides

FROM ALYSON BOOKS

AVAILABLE NOW

THE Q GUIDE TO THE GOLDEN GIRLS by Jim Colucci

THE Q GUIDE TO SOAP OPERAS by Daniel R. Coleridge

THE Q GUIDE TO BROADWAY by Seth Rudetsky

THE Q GUIDE TO OSCAR PARTIES
(and Other Awards Shows) by Joel Perry

THE Q GUIDE TO FIRE ISLAND by Steve Weinstein

THE Q GUIDE TO AMSTERDAM by Dara Colwell

THE Q GUIDE TO NYC PRIDE by Patrick Hinds

COMING SOON

THE Q GUIDE TO WINE AND COCKTAILS by Scott & Scott

THE Q GUIDE TO CLASSIC MONSTER MOVIES
by Douglas McEwan

LIFESTYLE

Q

OUT THERE

GUIDE

The Q Guide to

New York City Pride

**Stuff You Didn't Even Know You Wanted to
Know,** About the Landmarks, People, and
Events That Defined Queer Culture

[**patrick hinds**]

alyson books
NEW YORK

THIS TRADE PAPERBACK ORIGINAL IS PUBLISHED BY
ALYSON BOOKS,
245 W. 17TH ST., SUITE 1200
NEW YORK, NEW YORK 10011

DISTRIBUTION IN THE UNITED KINGDOM BY
TURNAROUND PUBLISHER SERVICES LTD.,
UNIT 3, OLYMPIA TRADING ESTATE,
COBURG ROAD, WOOD GREEN,
LONDON N22 6TZ ENGLAND.

FIRST EDITION: MAY 2007

07   08   09   10   **a**   10   9   8   7   6   5   4   3   2   1

ISBN 1-55583-994-0
ISBN-13 978-1-55583-994-9

LIBRARY OF CONGRESS CATALOGING-IN-PUBLICATION DATA
IS ON FILE.

This book is for my mother, Pam Parker,
who taught me to be proud.

Contents

Introduction

THE STONEWALL INN'S glassware was notoriously filthy. Smudged lipstick rings were imprinted around the rims like cracked fingerprints, and the warm remnants of watered down drinks often became ashtrays—a final resting place where cigarette-butt floaters and squeezed lemon wedges drowned slowly before being swooped up by the handful. Dropped by the bartender into a basin of hours-old water—cold and brown like a chocolate gazpacho—the glasses were hastily rinsed before being recycled back into service, carrying with them germs and little pieces of whatever else they had picked up along the way.

Like the glassware, the club itself festered. It was oppression, dark, and stuffy, and airless. A stale and salty sort of smog lingered while an ominous sense of foreboding skulked around like the Mafiosi who owned the place.

Those who were there remember that the music was what broke the tension—wailing that hovered above the smog, the foreboding, the Mafiosi. The music was what they went there for—why they endured the harassment at the door and the fear of arrest. It was the opportunity to dance in a room crowded with people, to sweat and laugh, kiss and hold hands without shame. It was the music that kept them going and made them believe that better days were ahead.

I discovered the Stonewall thirty-one years after history was made there. It was a perfect June day in Greenwich Village, the kind when beams of sunlight shine so directly that they seem almost to crash into the neighborhood, where the glow shatters and splashes the buildings like flecks of paint. I was twenty-one years old and two weeks out of college as I crossed Seventh Avenue South in search of the bar. I had done my homework, read the Stonewall books my mother, a lesbian, had given me when I told her I wanted to know more about gay and lesbian history. In the course of my reading, the riots had become something of a legend to me, and the bar, a birthplace, so I had gone in search of it that afternoon as if on a quest to unlock the mysteries of my heritage.

Twenty paces later I was standing right in front of it (now called the Stonewall Bar). Wedged as it was between a shoe outlet selling European knockoffs and a pet store where the doggies in the window scratched the glass and yelped at the sight of me, I would have missed the bar completely had I not been searching for it.

It was as though my body saw it first, bringing me up so short that I almost tripped, before my eyes caught up and immobilized me completely. I stood and gaped at the structure that had been made famous to me through pictures of the riot and noticed that, like all celebrities, it was smaller in real life than I had imagined it to be. With its big black door, red brick exterior, and a single window with a handwritten sign advertising "2-4-1 well cocktails 'till 9," I was overwhelmed by the unassumingness of it all. I wanted to jump up and down, point, grab passersby by the arm and shout, "Don't you know what this is? Don't you know what this place means?"

Instead, I walked two doors to the west of the bar, sat on a stoop—whose own story and historical significance I would discover in the years to follow—and tried to imagine what that place would have looked like one night in June 1969.

The space between the bar's entrance and the small park across the street, I noticed, was small and would have filled up quickly as people filed out of the place. With the crowd quickly numbering in the hundreds it would have been body to body in the street—people's arms, hands, legs touching as they gathered in the warm night air under the fluorescent street lights. A buzz of excitement and anger—a tangible sense of oneness—would have quickly circulated as the crowd began to feel its power. And then the *pop*—I always imagined that it was one magnificent surge of unified fury in which the situation outside the Stonewall Inn changed from a defiant demonstration to what became known as the Stonewall Riots.

I walked to the top of the stoop I was sitting on to get a better view of the landscape where the riots took place the same way the activist Craig Rodwell did on the night the riots began. I imagined Rodwell, at twenty-nine, standing where I now stood, confused and exhilarated, hoping as he watched the events unfold beneath his gaze that it was the moment he had been praying for—the moment when his gay brothers seized the opportunity to fight back. I grabbed the railing he would have grabbed when he threw his fist into the air and famously screamed the battle cry "Gay Power!" as the first rocks, bricks, and bottles were thrown at the police.

Over the course of the years that followed my first

visit to the Stonewall Inn, I became an unofficial professional student of New York City's queer history. I read the few books available. But, more interesting, I picked up knowledge in the unlikeliest of places, such as a Christopher Street coffee shop where invaluable nuggets of forgotten history sat in a window seat, locked away in the mind of a Stonewall-era old man who eagerly recounted forgotten tales to me once over afternoon tea. And I discovered the New York Public Library's International Gay Information Center, where untold stories of the gay movement's early days are archived and indexed, just waiting to be discovered.

One piece of information seemed to lead me to the next. I learned what happened at Julius', the city's oldest gay bar and the place where Edward Albee came across the sentence "Who's Afraid of Virginia Woolf?" scrawled on the bathroom door and decided to use it for the title of the play he was writing. I learned of the Mattachine Society, one of New York's oldest organizations for gays and lesbians, and how its early activism paved the way for groups such as Gay Activists Alliance, Gay Liberation Front, and even ACT UP (AIDS Coalition to Unleash Power). I discovered the Christopher Street Liberation Day March and how it ultimately became what we know today as Pride. I discovered Larry Kramer and how, love him or hate him, he undeniably gave his life to the gay community in the name of AIDS activism, awareness, and education.

As I connected the dots I began to see how the people, places, and events I had been studying came together to make up the queer history of this city. And while in no way attempting to write a definitive history,

I have tried, in the pages that follow, to present what I have uncovered over the last six years in my exhaustive if informal excavation of New York's fabulously queer past. It is a tribute to those who, by simply living through it, paved the way.

The Q Guide to

NYC Pride

Downtown's Secret Gay Underworld

QUOTE

"So many seemingly ordinary spots in the village have quiet but significant stories that were once so secret they have almost been forgotten altogether."

IT SEEMS easy to believe that the gay history of New York City began on the warm night of June 28, 1969, with the riots at the Stonewall Inn. Of course, that isn't true. There have been gay people on this island as long as there have been people here. And for them, the riots were a turning point, a beautiful moment of revelation when they realized their power as never before.

Images of the riots at Stonewall—angry and excited boys and men standing toe to toe with police officers for the first time in history—have become famous. But years before that night, an entire gay underworld existed here, which laid the groundwork for such an uprising. It was a world of forbidden bars and underground restaurants, late-night cruising on downtown streets, and clandestine meetings in basement apartments where the country's earliest gay activists plotted our community's way out of living in the shadows.

The importance of the people and places of the pre-Stonewall era in New York City is often overlooked. But it was among them that momentum slowly gathered and the stage was set for the riots that would change the course of LGBT history.

Pre-Stonewall Landmarks

The stoop at 177 Christopher Street is brown and ugly, seven cement steps leading up to a heavy-looking wooden door whose black paint, though lacquered and shiny, is uneven in sections and chipped around the hinges. It is an unimpressive location in comparison to others on the historic street that winds its way through the heart of Greenwich Village, one of the world's oldest and most renowned gay neighborhoods. Unimpressive, that is, unless you know the stoop's history. If it could talk, it would tell passersby her role in the famed Stonewall Riots of 1969, that it was from her top step that a young activist named Craig Rodwell screamed the words "Gay Power!" which would be remembered as the battle cry that started the riots that sparked the gay revolution.

Many of the village's restaurants, apartment buildings, bars, and coffee shops—seemingly ordinary locales that people pass every day without giving them a second thought—are teaming with a queer history just waiting to be uncovered.

Mama's Chick & Rib

On certain nights in the late 1950s,[*] in a medium-sized place called Mama's Chick & Rib, at 39 Greenwich Avenue, on the corner of Charles Street, Jack, a tall, good-looking waiter, would lock the restaurant's door before simultaneously turning on the heating and air-conditioning units in order to fog up the windows. It would be one of those rare nights when the restaurant, always open until the wee hours of the morning, was full of familiar faces—friends and regulars—and he was sure that nobody was an undercover cop looking to raid the place because it was a gay watering hole, and he would turn the music up and the lights down. That was the cue, if you were a patron of the establishment and lucky enough to be there on such a night, that a little bit of dancing would be okay, and maybe some hand holding or even kissing—a display of public affection so taboo it was unheard of at the time—as long as it was discreet and didn't persist for too long.

Certainly Mama's wasn't the only place in town where the gays of the day could go to congregate, but it was the only establishment of the few known businesses catering to a gay clientele that wasn't owned and operated by the Mafia—places that, according to Tree, a Village resident of the time, "charged you to get in, watered down the drinks, and roughed you up if you got too drunk." And so those in the know hung out at Mama's, a gay speakeasy in its own right whose owner, Mama, had to

TIP For nearly thirty years,* a framed picture of Jack hung in the barber shop where he got his hair cut, around the corner from Mama's.

pay off the local police precinct on a weekly basis in order to stay in business, and waited for those magical nights when Mama would leave early, and Jack, the cute waiter, would lock the door behind her.

The Corner

In the heart of the West Village in downtown Manhattan a few blocks west of Washington Square Park, the onetime site of the city's gallows and mass paupers' grave, and a few blocks east of the building that would become the Stonewall Inn, the site of the riots that began the gay revolution,† Greenwich Avenue and Christopher Street converge at an unimpressive tree-lined intersection two blocks south of where Mama's Chick & Rib once stood. The northwest corner of the intersection, with its dirty and cracked gum strewn sidewalk, seems nondescript and unremarkable, an unlikely location for anything significant to have happened. But like many seemingly ordinary spots in the Village, the Corner, as it was once known, has a quiet but significant story that was once so secret that it has almost been forgotten all together.

The Corner's story began in the 1950s, when tales of Greenwich Village, "America's bohemia," as it would come to be known, spread across the country. Stories of misfits and outcasts told by Village residents such as Jack Kerouac, Bob Dylan, and Allen Ginsberg, to name just a few, piqued the interest of the nation's queers, a set of misfits and outcasts in their own right, and drew them to New York City in such numbers that it quickly became the metropolis with the largest gay population in the United States. What they found when they got there, however, was not the freedom they had hoped for, but rather a city that, more aggressively than any other, kept its homosexuals in line by ruling with what would today be considered a sort of martial law.* The New York State Liquor Authority (SLA), in addition to threatening to close down any establishment that knowingly served a group of three or more homosexuals, had classified homosexuals among the "lewd and dissolute," thus making their presence in a bar and thus the bar itself by definition "disorderly and subject to closure."† In New York City, the act of dressing in drag was illegal, because of a nineteenth-century antilabor ordinance condemning any person "wearing fewer than three articles of clothing appropriate to their sex." New York was also the first city to create a police vice squad to observe—and entrap—homosexuals in the places where they gathered; this translated into the routine raiding of known gay bars and bathhouses, where over a hundred men were arrested each week. Along with these arrests—the records of which were sometimes published in newspa-

Tree

I'VE BEEN TENDING and managing bars* at gay establishments in the Village for thirty years now (and have been living in the same one-bedroom apartment in Chelsea for the same amount of time—it was $120 a month when I moved in!).

I came to Mama's Chick & Rib as a manager and waiter in 1958 and worked there for a good three years. Mama, whose name was actually Helena, but we never called her that, owned the place with her husband—we called him Papa; I don't think I ever actually knew his name. She was quite a character for a little old Greek lady. I remember that she had a mole on her chin with little brown hairs sprouting out of it and that she only wore two dresses—one blue, one black. I used to tell people that when she washed one of them we would have onion soup for a week.

She always wore a string of pearls around her neck. She insisted they were real and we believed her. They were her one luxury item and the only thing I ever saw inspire a sense of vanity in her.

I have no idea how the place came to be a gay hangout—it was one long before I came on board there. Most of the staff was gay and Mama referred to us as "her boys." I'm sure she knew the sort of clientele we catered to, but it was never talked about with her or Papa. That is except for the occasion or two when Mama pulled me aside and, making a crude gesture with her hand like she was shoving something into her mouth, asked me in her thick Greek accent, "My-a boys-a don-a do that, a-right?" Recognizing the universal symbol for oral sex on a man, I replied, "Ah, yeah, we do, Mama." I remember her looking puzzled, throwing her hands in the air, and walking away.

Though Mama's was known for its subpar food and for the commingling of rats and cockroaches, it was a twenty-four-hour joint that I was pretty much allowed to run by myself when Mama left for the night. Jack and I learned the trick of turning on the air-conditioning and heating at the same time to fog the windows one afternoon when a repairman was working and did it by accident. Over time we became so comfortable with how gay the place had become after hours that we became remarkably bold with anyone we felt might disturb us. I remember that it got to the point where if a straight couple tried to come in late at night one of us would tell the guy that we were full but he was welcome to come back without his girlfriend if he wanted to. And a couple of times they did.

As mornings dawned, we would pass a box around for everyone to put money in which we in turn would put in the till. Mama would come in the next morning, see that the register was full, and never asked me any questions.

pers—came the automatic registration as a sex of-
fender—and queers were defined as such—which usually resulted in the man's immediate firing from a government job, if he held one, and the revocation of any
professional licenses he held.

It was difficult and dangerous to be openly gay in the
sixties in New York, even though it seemed that the
peace and love movement was thriving for everybody
else. But queers are survivors. And despite the best efforts of the authorities to keep them separate, a group
not only disenfranchised by the city but also alienated
from each other, they found a way—and a place—to
meet. They found the Corner. Though it is sometimes
described as the premiere cruising spot for gay men in
the sixties, more important is that the Corner (now
home to an independent T-shirt shop) is remembered as
the first place where gay men could go to meet each
other out in the open. Thus, on this unimpressive corner, since traversed by countless millions of unknowing
tourists and residents, was the spot where a sense of
community and oneness—which would be integral in
anchoring and guiding the gay community thorough the
battles that lay ahead—was born.

Julius', 159 West Tenth Street

On the unseasonably warm afternoon* of April 26, 1966,
four gay men, dressed uncharacteristically in dark navy
suits, walked west on West Tenth street and picked up
the pace until they reached the heavy wooden door of
the bar called, simply, Julius'. Dick Leitsch, president of
the New York chapter of the Mattachine Society, held

the door for his three companions, John Timmons, a Mattachine colleague, and Craig Rodwell and Randy Wicker, two ex-Mattachine members who had left the group in frustration because they felt it wasn't focused enough on public outreach. Trailing behind these three were a few members of the press invited along by Leitsch; to his surprise, they actually showed up to document the gay community's first ever militant action. But Julius' wasn't the group's first stop of the day.

The trio's idea was simple, or so they thought: to challenge the legality of the SLA ban on serving alcohol to homosexuals by visiting a number of bars and restaurants in the course of the afternoon and demanding to be served. The law had been on the books since 1933—just one of many instituted to control the sale and consumption of alcohol after Prohibition was repealed that year. The wording of the law included homosexuals among the "lewd and dissolute" whose mere presence would deem an establishment "disorderly and subject to closure."* The law made it legal to threaten with closure any establishment that didn't go along with the homophobic stricture of refusing to serve gay men. It had been enforced since the city began "cleaning up" in preparation to host the 1964 World's Fair. And so all around the city once well-known gay bars—Julius' included—hung signs above their doors that read "If You Are Gay, Please Go Away," and began enforcing a policy that every man who entered must be accompanied by a woman. The management of Julius' had even gone as far as to throw Rodwell out of the establishment one night the year before because he wore a gay liberation button on his coat.

"Taking the button off wasn't an option," Rodwell recalled later. "I had to leave."*

Leitsch had set his sights particularly on the city's most notoriously homophobic establishment, the Ukrainian-American Restaurant on St. Mark's Place in the East Village. There the sign above the door sign outdid the gay bars and others prohibited from serving homosexuals by declaring, "We don't serve faggots."†

The group would announce to the manager of an establishment that they were homosexuals and that it was against state regulation to knowingly serve them a drink, but then one of them would declare: "I, however, want to order a scotch and soda."‡ When denied service they intended to "file a complaint against the bar and the SLA for violating their constitutional rights to both free assembly and equal accommodation."**

The group endured a number of frustrating misadventures that afternoon. At the Ukrainian-American Restaurant, they arrived only to find the place closed for the day, as the manager had been tipped of by a member of the press. At their next stop, the Howard Johnson's, the group received a plan-thwarting laugh from the manager, who, unwilling to get involved in any legal situation, claimed to know of no regulation against serving homosexuals. Just to be on the safe side, he served the group—including the journalists—a round of drinks on the house so as to avoid any legal transaction. The group then left the HoJo and headed over to the Waikiki, on Greenwich Avenue and Tenth Street, where they were again served their drinks on the house. "Still sort of terrified and now getting drunk,"†† Rodwell recounted, they went into a huddle and decided that Julius', just a few blocks away, was the place where they knew for sure they could manipulate their plan into action.

Julius' had opened during Prohibition as a speakeasy and by the late 1950s had become established as New York City's first bar catering primarily to homosexuals. With its shadowy lighting and dingy walls lined with water-stained black-and-white photos of actresses nobody had ever heard of, it gave Leitsch cause, as he made his way through the crowd to the bar, to be disappointed embarrassed, even in front of the press group he had invited, that this was the place where his group was going to make their stand. It got even worse when he made his announcement and then ordered the round of drinks and watched the bartender, without a moment's hesitation, line up the glasses to fill them.

Refusing to be foiled for a fourth time in one afternoon, Leitsch pushed back through the crowd and found the manager, to whom he explained the importance of what he and his group were trying to do that day. The manager reluctantly agreed to play along with the plan, on condition that the Mattachine Society would help the bar get legal assistance in another matter, then explained the situation to the bartender. The bartender, annoyed, rolled his eyes before taking the drinks away and announcing that he couldn't serve the four men standing there, saying, "I think it's the law."*

It took the SLA four days to respond to the extensive media coverage garnered by what the *New York Times* called "the sip in." And when the state did react, it was only to slough the problem off to another of the city's departments. "This might be a matter for the Commission on Human Rights,"† the SLA chairman, Donald

Hostetter, said. The Commission on Human Rights did get involved and ultimately found that denial of service to a homosexual would "come within the bounds"* of a law on the books in the city that outlawed discrimination on the basis of sex. The discriminatory laws were immediately repealed.

Julius', already an institution in the West Village, became an instant landmark and four years later was featured in the film *The Boys in the Band*. It has closed just once in its more than fifty years of operation, and that was only briefly, for renovation.

The Oscar Wilde Memorial Bookshop

In the summer of 1966,† Craig Rodwell boarded a ferry in Sayville, New York, bound for Fire Island. Having secured a job cleaning rooms at a popular gay hotel, he knew that a summer away from the city would do him good. He was fed up with the state of activism and frustrated that his ideas weren't being taken seriously by the powers that be within the gay groups in New York City.

His latest idea was about visibility. He had proposed to the New York chapter of the Mattachine Society that they rent a storefront in one of the popular gay neighborhoods and make it the group's headquarters. He was sure that the move would attract new members by making the organization feel less like a clandestine operation with something to hide. The group would also be able to publish pamphlets, magazines, and books concerning the homophile movement and more readily distribute them to the public. When his proposal was shot down by the society's board, he knew he was done with the group, that whatever ties he still had with them had to be cut forever.

If the Mattachine Society wasn't interested in his idea, he'd do it himself. Rodwell wasn't much of a reader—never had the attention span for books—but he knew that what gay and lesbian people needed then more than anything else was a legitimate business that lent itself to browsing, mingling, meeting, and talking. A bookshop seemed the perfect idea. In order for it to work, Rodwell knew that his business would have to fly in the face of backroom sex and porn shops that stayed in business by calling themselves bookstores, though often there was often not a single book or periodical on the premises. He conceived of his new bookshop as a street-level store with a big plate-glass window that would show the world that it was a gay establishment with nothing to hide.

It took two summers of cleaning rooms, doing laundry, washing dishes, and doing whatever other odd jobs he could find on Fire Island to raise the money he needed to open his store. On Thanksgiving Day in 1967, the Oscar Wilde Memorial Bookshop—named for the nineteenth-century playwright who was convicted of practicing sodomy and was imprisoned—opened in a small storefront at 291 Mercer Street, in Greenwich Village. It was not only* the world's first gay bookstore but was also probably the world's first business to cater specifically to gay men and lesbians that was not involved with sex or alcohol. Rodwell hadn't read a single title on the shelves.

TIP Rodwell, during his interviews with the historian Martin Duberman for Duberman's book *Stonewall,* alluded to having been part of a small-time drug ring on Fire Island while working to save money to open the bookstore. At one point he asked Duberman to turn the tape recorder off so he could speak off the record on the subject.

Rodwell's refusal to sell any pornographic materials or materials that were offensive to women or minorities led him into financial difficulties almost immediately. "I wanted to have good literature that represented homosexuality in a good light," he told the activist Kay Tobin for her 1972 book, *Gay Crusaders.* Rodwell refused to buckle under the financial strain.

In 1973, as the bookshop's revenues increased, Rodwell moved it to a row house on Christopher Street, a block away from the famed Stonewall Inn. In the window hung a sticker with the message "Gay Is Good." Though the bookshop was eventually sold (Rodwell died in 1994), it has remained quietly in the same location for the past thirty-five years.

Almost overnight after its Thanksgiving Day open-

TIP Craig Rodwell, when he was still owner of the Oscar Wilde Memorial Bookshop, was the target of a stalker who sent threatening letters, including death threats, to both his home and the bookshop.

ing, the Oscar Wilde became the first unofficial GLBT community center anywhere. In its early days, the bookshop was called "the clearinghouse for individuals and organizations supporting homosexual law reform in New York State." It was also the headquarters for a small activist group put together by Rodwell called the Homophile Youth Movement in Neighborhoods (HYMN). Rodwell wrote the group's newsletter, *The Hymnal*, and distributed it at the bookshop.

Over the years the bookshop has experienced its fair share of controversy. In the late 1970s, Rodwell engaged in a public feud with the author and activist Larry Kramer over Rodwell's refusal to stock Kramer's novel *Faggots* because he found it offensive. In another instance, the bookshop was vandalized one afternoon by a man who threw a brick through its front window during business hours. In the wake of that event a full-time security guard was hired to be on hand in case of future attacks.

Q-TIP

According to the shop's new owner, Kim Brinster, every year since the death of her son, in 1994, Marion Rodwell would come down to the Oscar Wilde Bookshop. Before leaving, she would walk to the center of the store where she would stand as if presenting herself on a pedestal and say, "Now this place is classy!"

The Organizations
The Mattachine Society of New York

On a breezy October night* in 1950, in the Silver Lake district of Los Angeles, five men gathered in the sensibly decorated living room of Harry Hay. Just by being alone together, the men—Chuck Rowland, Bob Hull, Dale Jennings, Konrad Stevens, John Gruber, and Hay—all of whom were gay, were breaking the law. At the time it was illegal in the state of California for more than two homosexuals to gather at one time.

Hay, an attractive man known for his muscular build, had been married since 1938, though he'd known he was gay and had been having affairs with men since his teenage years. By the late 1940s, Hay, a born leader who was fed up with the inaction of American homosexuals, had an ominous vision of what would become of them all if someone didn't step forward and organize them. As he later told Jonathan Katz, the author of *Gay American History*: "The country, it seemed to me,* was beginning to move toward fascism and McCarthyism; the Jews wouldn't be used as a scapegoat this time—the painful example of Germany was still too clear to us. The Black organizations were already pretty successfully looking out for their interests. It was obvious McCarthy was setting up the pattern for a new scapegoat, and it was going to be us—Gays. We had to organize, we had to move, we had to get started."

Getting started was precisely his motivation for calling the meeting at his house that night in October. Hay told the assembled group of an idea he'd been trying to get off the ground since 1948 to found "a service and welfare organization devoted to the protection and improvement of Society's Androgynous Minority."† (He used the term "androgynous minority" intentionally to avoid using the word "homosexual.") The five men agreed, and the organization was born. It was named the Mattachine Society after Mattacino, a masked jester in Italian theater who, unlike the usual courtiers, would speak the truth to the king.

The Mattachine Society's New York chapter was organized soon thereafter—though it's important to note the often-forgotten fact that Mattachine Society was not New York's first gay rights group. (The city's first gay organization, according to Molly McGarry and Fred

Kim Brinster, Owner of Oscar Wilde Bookshop, on Preserving a Legacy

I CAME TO New York City in 1979 to get a master's degree in religious education at Fordham. Like all lesbian and gay people, I didn't take long to make a sort of second home of the West Village. I discovered the Oscar Wilde Memorial Bookshop quickly—it was still the only bookshop of its kind back in those days—and I was a customer there for years. And then in the eighties I became a letter carrier in the neighborhood and was responsible for delivering all of the books to Craig Rodwell at the bookshop.

In 1994 when Craig was diagnosed with stomach cancer, he sold the bookshop to a man named Bill Offenbaker, who did the best he could with it for a few years before selling the property to two women. The two women, whose names have been lost to history, unable to make the business profitable, sold the business back to Bill in 1996. I was in Houston at the time managing a LGBT bookstore called Lobo and heard through the bookseller grapevine that Oscar Wilde was in danger of closing. The owner of Lobo immediately negotiated a deal with Bill to purchase the store sight unseen. I was handed the keys to the space and flown back to New York, where I was to be the bookshop manager.

We had to close the space for three weeks to renovate—the place was a disaster. We knocked down a few walls and repainted others, installed professional lighting, and we had to get rid of a bathtub and a sink (the store space had originally been converted from two studio apartments). It would have been a disastrously expensive undertaking if it hadn't been for the construction crew, who gave us great deals out of dedication to preserving the historic space.

Despite a friendly competition with A Different Light, a sort of gay superstore in Chelsea, things at the renovated Oscar Wilde Bookshop (we dropped "Memorial" from the name in 1996) were pretty smooth until 2003, when it was purchased by Deacon Maccubbin. Deacon, owner of the Lambda Rising gay bookstore chain, with headquarters in Washington, DC, felt that the bookshop was a landmark and was committed to keeping it open whether it was profitable or not.

In February of 2006, having run the place for ten years, Deacon, knowing my commitment to the bookshop, agreed to sell the store to me. Though, as with all bookstores, the profit margin is not huge, my commitment to the store is unwavering. All of us, especially my manager, Cecilia, wear many hats in order to keep it going. We live tight here at Oscar Wilde, but we're all passionate about preserving the store's legacy.*

TIP Harry Hay, the founder of the Mattachine Society (born on April 9, 1912), was at one point romantically connected to Will Geer, the actor who played Grandpa Walton on *The Waltons*. He is also said to have been the first person to apply the term "minority" to homosexuals.

Wasserman, the authors of *Becoming Visible*, was the Veterans' Benevolent Association, which was founded in 1945. The group held social functions that were often attended by up to five hundred people. The group was also known to help gays who were arrested, or discriminated against because of their homosexuality.)

In 1950, a faction of Mattachine's more militant members started the magazine *One*. *One*'s intentionally unapologetic tone—it announced on its cover that it represented "The Homosexual Viewpoint"—challenged the Mattachine Society's generally assimilationist stance. *One* was not the first publication to come from the society—it had been circulating leaflets as well as a pamphlet called *The Mattachine Review* for a couple of years by then—but it was the most controversial. When its subscriber list more than doubled, to 5,000, in its second year, it was also the most widely read.

In its early years, the New York Mattachine chapter was respected by its members for the work it did to further the cause of gay rights. Together with the Washington, DC, chapter, New York adopted a formal resolution in 1965 declaring that homosexuality was not an illness, as was widely held by psychologists of the day. The resolution read: "In absence of valid evidence to the contrary, homosexuality is not a sickness, disturbance, or other pathology in any sense, but is merely a preference, orientation, or propensity, on [a] par with, and different in kind from, heterosexuality."*

In the wake of the excitement and empowerment that came along with the Stonewall Riots, in the 1970s, Mattachine got a phone call from another lesbian couple. It was an invitation of sorts to have lunch with two other lesbian couples—four couples in total—to formally discuss the idea of starting a social club for lesbians. Martin and Lyon agreed to the meeting immediately, as they, too, were tired of seedy bars being the only places that lesbians seemed able to meet each other and socialize. In much the same way as had happened with the Mattachine Society, the Daughters of Bilitis (DOB), the country's first lesbian organization, was born that evening in a living room. Also like the Mattachine Society, in the beginning DOB functioned as a clandestine operation. The word "daughters" was meant to evoke association with other sororal organizations such as Daughters of the American Revolution, and the name "Bilitis" was inspired by the book *Songs of Bilitis* (*Chansons de Bilitis*) by a French writer, Pierre Louÿs, containing prose poems about between women, purportedly translated from the Greek. Years later Del Martin

TIP The original Bilitis was supposedly a poetess who lived on the island of Lesbos in the time of Sappho.

recalled,[*] "We thought that Daughters of Bilitis would sound like any other women's lodge....Bilitis would mean something to us, but not to any outsider. If anyone asked us, we could always say we belong to a poetry club" (Martin and Lyon, *Lesbian Woman*). The group also encouraged its members to use pseudonyms.

Two years later, in 1958, Martin and Lyon, eager for DOB to expand, asked Gittings to open a chapter in New York City. Despite the fact that she lived in Philadelphia and knew that the commute to New York would be a challenge, Barbara Gittings accepted the offer and opened the New York chapter—the city's first organization geared toward the needs of the lesbian community.

Perhaps the most significant achievement of DOB was the publication of its magazine *The Ladder*, which began in 1956 with a national circulation of several hundred. Gittings, who was the editor of the magazine from 1963 to 1966, recalled how important *The Ladder* was to closeted lesbians of the day: "They might still be isolated geographically,[†] but as long as they knew that a thousand miles away there was a group, as long as they could

TIP Del Martin and Phyllis Martin, the cofounders of Daughters of Bilitis, were the first same-sex couple to receive a government sanctioned marriage license in the United States, in San Francisco, in 2004.

occasionally get some kind of publication, it was so much better than simply living in their own little cocoon" (Katz, *Gay American History*).

The New York chapter of DOB and Mattachine–New York often joined together in what they called "common cause." Along with two other groups, in 1963 they established the Eastern Regional Conference of Homophile Organizations (ERCHO). ERCHO held monthly meetings and annual conferences where activists came together to share ideas, create alliances, and plan joint demonstrations. The creation of ERCHO was a monumental first step in establishing the lesbian and gay community as a political force. While Mattachine–New York and DOB had always worked well together, as the women's movement began to grow, it became clear to the DOB membership that the men of Mattachine had little interest in women's issues.

Though the group was influential throughout the 1950s and 1960s, it became divided and ultimately broke

TIP In the mid-1960s, the New York chapter of Daughters of Bilitis elected a black vice president, named Ernestine Eckstein (a pseudonym). It marked the first time an office in any of the existing homophile organizations was held by a person of color.

up in the 1970s over the debate of whether the group should focus more on issues of feminism or on gay rights. However, a chapter of Daughters of Bilitis survives to this day in Cambridge, Massachusetts.

Q-Review

Harry Hay. Often referred to as "the father of gay rights in America," Hay was the cofounder of the Mattachine Society. Hay also founded the Radical Faeries in 1979, a political group whose core belief is that gay men are spiritually different from other people. Hay, the subject of a 2002 documentary, *Hope Along the Wind: The Story of Harry Hay*, died of lung cancer in San Francisco in 2002.

Dick Leitsch. President of the Mattachine Society of New York from 1965 through the early 1970s. Though an important figure in New York city activism, Leitsch was criticized for his passive response to the Stonewall Riots.

Del Martin and Phyllis Martin. Martin and Lyons, a couple for over fifty-three years, were the cofounders of the country's first lesbian organization, Daughters of Bilitis. They also founded the Lyon-Martin Women's Health Services Center in San Francisco in 1979. Both women were appointed delegates to the 1995 White House Conference on Aging. Convened by President Bill Clinton on February 17, it was a program designed to strengthen the "social safety net" for aging Americans.

Barbara Gittings. One of New York City's earliest lesbian activists. Gittings opened the New York chapter of Daughters of Bilitis in 1958.

CHAPTER TWO

The Boiling Point

QUOTE

"When I saw the group of people gathered outside Stonewall, I immediately knew this was the spark we had been waiting for for years.…There was a feeling in the air [that] this time was different."

—Craig Rodwell

YEARS LATER, when the world began to truly recognize the importance of the events that took place at the Stonewall Inn during the early-morning hours of June 28, 1969, people would recall that it was warm out that night. They would remember that Judy Garland, a gay icon, had been laid to rest earlier that day and would wonder whether the Stonewall had been unusually crowded because people felt a need to go out and celebrate Garland's life.

And then, as the big picture came into focus, they would recall just how insufferable life was for gay New Yorkers by the end of the 1960s. How the Mafia ran all of the city's gay bars—the only places where it was "safe" for gays to congregate, yet where patrons were often pushed around and overcharged for watered-down drinks. How raids by the police were so common and arrests so prevalent that officers usually knew their arrestees by name. They would recall a world in which gender expression was illegal and cruising could get you thrown in jail. And they would understand that the city's gays were being pushed toward a boiling point. A boiling point that came just after 1 A.M., when Officer Seymour Pine entered the Stonewall Inn with his subordinate officers and told the doorman, "We're taking the place."[*]

The History

It's hard to believe that the area now known as Greenwich Village was considered a remote locale to the Dutch who settled in the lower part of the island of Manhattan. In fact, according to Carter's *Stonewall: The Riots That Sparked the Gay Revolution*, Dutch settlers first began moving into the remote area to escape from the plague—so many that "it became necessary to lay down roads."[†] Over time, Greenwich Village became known for its sense of community and for its vigilance in resisting the modernizing changes that were transforming old New York into the thriving metropolis it is today. By the early 1900s, the Village had become known as an artistic and bohemian Mecca.

But by the early 1930s, Prohibition and other factors had brought change to Greenwich Village. The bohemia once known for its clubs and bars had, with the outlawing of liquor, become a hotbed for a new type of hangout—the tearoom. One of the better-known tearooms, considered scandalous because it drew a largely lesbian clientele, was Bonni's Stone Wall, which had gone in at 53 Christopher Street after the wall connecting the building to the stable next door was knocked down and the two houses were connected to become one. Bonni's Stonewall, Carter speculates, was given its name as a sort of coded invitation to the lesbians of the day, for the name was an allusion to the autobiography of the pseudonymous Mary Casal, *The Stone Wall: An Autobiography*;* published in 1930, it depicted her life as a lesbian in rural New England.

Ultimately, the tearoom survived the hard years of Prohibition and was expanded into a restaurant before undergoing a name change and becoming Bonni's Stonewall Inn, a popular reception and banquet hall. In the early 1950s it became the Stonewall Inn Restaurant for a few years, before being gutted by a fire. The space sat vacant until 1967, when a local mobster known as "Fat Tony" Lauria, looking to capitalize on the scant number of places where the large number of neighborhood gays could gather, went against the wishes of his father and opened the place as a gay bar, the Stonewall Inn.

The Riot

A little after 1 A.M.* on June 28, 1969, Officer Seymour Pine made his decision: it was time to go in to the Stonewall Inn. Officer Pine—accompanied by four other plainclothes policemen, two patrolmen, and a city detective—had been waiting since midnight in Christopher Park, across the street from the bar, for two female undercover agents who had been sent in earlier to come back out with information. When they had failed to return, Pine, fearing for their safety as well as for the integrity of the raid he had so painstakingly put together, decided it was time to make his move. And so he and his team crossed Christopher Street and confronted the bar's doorman, announcing that they were the police and that they were taking the place.

Pine, the officer in charge of Manhattan's First Division of Public Morals, was sick of the control the Mafia had over city bars and the inherent corruption it led to. In interviews he has given since the riots, Pine has insisted that his targets that night were the Mafiosi who owned and operated the Stonewall as well as the bar's employees. But when the agents got rough while trying to separate the drag queens from the rest of the patrons—a common practice that culminated in a physical check because dressing in drag was still an arrestable offense in those days—people began to resist.

Outside Stonewall, at 1:30 A.M.—the peak time for going out on the town in the West Village—a crowd made up of both those who had been kicked out of the club and curious passersby making their way through

Sheridan Square amassed and quickly began to number in the hundreds. It was significant that the crowd hung around and grew, for it was the first time in the history of a bar raid that those who had escaped being arrested didn't disappear into the night feeling lucky and grateful for having escaped but instead stayed on the spot. Though the people in the crowd at first seemed practically jovial in their defiance, the attitude quickly shifted as the patrons who had been detained were dragged or shoved out of the club and into paddy wagons. The first act of serious violence occurred when a cop clubbed a drag queen after she had tapped him on the head with her purse as he tried to shove her out of the club.

The incident most often credited with starting the actual riot occurred just a few minutes after the clubbing of the drag queen and centered around an unidentified woman known historically only as "the Stonewall Lesbian." It has been speculated that she was at the bar visiting a friend who worked at the club when the police raided the place. Accounts of how she ended up outside the bar vary, but almost all witnesses to the event remember seeing her standing outside the inn and being shoved by a cop. When she protested the harassment she was struck in the face with a billy club and fell to the ground. For the gathered crowd, that was the breaking point; picking up whatever they could find, they began throwing bottles, rocks, and even change at the police. Fearing for their safety, the police barricaded themselves inside the Stonewall Inn.

The Stonewall Lesbian never came forward after the riots to take credit for her role in them, and she was never

Storme DeLarverie, the Stonewall Lesbian. Did This Woman Start the Riot?

WHEN ASKED how she ended up at Stonewall on that fateful night in June of 1969, Storme DeLarverie says, "It was an accident." If so, it is perhaps the most significant accident in gay and lesbian history, as many credit her presence and subsequent involvement in the rebellion as being the spark that ignited the riots.

Born in New Orleans in 1926 to a black mother who was a servant and a white father, DeLarverie was raised on music. In 1936 she began a career as a professional big band singer touring the country, "with my long hair and high heels." With her turn as the emcee of the legendary Jewel Box Revue—a touring company of female impersonators that was America's first integrated female-impersonation show—she hit her stride. The show's only woman, DeLarverie abandoned the hair and the heels and dressed as a man making her one of the country's earliest known drag kings. She is proud of the distinction of emceeing the show for fifteen years, remembering fondly, "It was advertised as 'twenty-five men and one girl,' but it was really thirty-two men and me."

On June 27, 1969, after a show at the legendary Apollo Theater in Harlem, DeLarverie made her way downtown to the Stonewall. "I always went down to the gay bars in the Village when I was in town," she said. "I rarely went to the women's bars, but I always stopped by the Stonewall and others like it. I liked to see if I could help the boys out in any way."

Dressed "as any gay man would be," in a lapel jacket and slacks, her short hair slicked down in the style she wore it in for the show, she happened upon the Stonewall just as the crowd was starting to gather. Standing against the fence surrounding Christopher Park, she watched the scene unfold until she noticed the police bullying a man near the bar's entrance. As she made her way to the man's side to help him, a police officer grabbed her shoulder and said, "Move along."

"As politely as I could," she recalls, "I said, 'Just a minute, officer, I'm trying to help this man.' He then yelled, 'I said move along, faggot.' I think he thought I was a boy. When I refused, he raised his nightstick and clubbed me in the face." That was when the crowd surged and started pelting the cops with anything that came to hand. The beating left DeLarverie with a black eye, and ultimately she required fourteen stitches in her face.

When asked whether she was aware of the legend of the Stonewall Lesbian whose beating incited the riot, DeLarverie, now eight-five, smiled proudly and said, "Yes, I am. They were talking about me." And when asked why she never came forward before to claim her place in history, she answered shyly, "It was never any of anyone's business."

After the riots, she continued on with her life in show business before retiring in New York City's Chelsea neighborhood. She has since worked as a body guard, head of security, and fundraiser for charities benefiting battered women and children.*

identified. It was assumed that she had died shortly there-after without ever realizing her significance.

Rodwell, in an interview with the historian Martin Duberman for Duberman's book *Stonewall*, disagrees with the idea that any one thing can be credited with starting the riot. "When I saw the group of people gath-ered outside Stonewall, I immediately knew this was the spark we had been waiting for for years....There was a feeling in the air [that] this time was different....It was one of those moments in history when everything comes together. It has to do with the weather, the time of the day, and the week, and whose around."

The rioting began with the smashing of all of Stonewall's windows. Things escalated when the police, in fear for their lives and awaiting backup, locked them-

TIP
Gay Street, a street integral to the success of the Stonewall Riots because of the curve it forms and its location off of Christopher Street—is not an allusion to the village's gay community, as is commonly thought. Rather, the street was named for the abolitionist attorney Sidney Howard Gay in the late 1800s.

selves inside the club. A group of enraged street youths, determined to confront the cops face to face inside the Stonewall, ripped out a parking meter and used it as a battering ram on the club's front door. Soon thereafter, as the crowd swelled to over a thousand people, a group began throwing Molotov cocktails into the club in an effort to set the place on fire and smoke the police out. The riot ended up as a street battle between the protesters and the city's riot police and lasted until around 3 A.M. Sunday morning—a full twenty-six hours. Smatterings of uprisings continued throughout the week.

"The second night was the worst," Rodwell reflected. With reports of a taxi cab almost overturned by rioters as it tried to turn onto Greenwich Avenue, trash cans being set on fire all around Greenwich Village, and the hundreds of glass bottles being thrown at the police from a group that had gathered in Christopher Park, it was certainly the most violent. The scene inspired the gay poet and Village resident Allen Ginsberg to tell a reporter, famously, "They've lost that wounded look that fags all had ten years ago."[*]

It was Rodwell who had the foresight to call the press. The New York *Daily News* (a liberal paper at the time), the *New York Times*, and the *Village Voice* all covered the riots. The *Voice* offices were just a few doors down from the Stonewall and their reporter got a first-hand account of the riot's first night. The story in the *Daily News*, headlined "Homo Nest Raided; Queen Bees Stinging Mad," made a homophobic mockery of the event. The *Times*, though it was making an effort at the time to be more aware of gay issues, did not cover the riot immediately. When they finally did run a story a few days later, the coverage was relegated to a few short paragraphs on the inside pages. The most comprehensive coverage was provided by the *Village Voice*'s two cover stories, the first one appearing the day after the riot. Even though the *Voice*'s reporting was often sensationalized and misinformed, Tom Willenbecher, a historian who was at the riot,[†] later wrote, "Despite its sensationalism, the *Voice* article may well have been what elevated the riots from a typical street brawl in atypical costume to an historical event."

TIP

- There are over 10,000 bodies* buried beneath what is now Washington Square Park—formerly the site of the city's gallows and a burial ground for paupers' graves.
- Edgar Allan Poe was at one time a resident of Christopher Street. He has been called America's first bohemian.
- The winding streets of the West Village follow the footpaths of the natives who were here before the Dutch. The paths were dug out and paved over.
- The West Village is the only neighborhood north of Wall Street that doesn't follow New York City's grid pattern.
- Christopher Street is the longest street in the West Village.
- Christopher Park, the triangular park across the street from Stonewall, was at one time the site of a neighborhood tenement building. It burned to the ground in the early 1900s, killing more than forty people. When the city tried to rebuild the structure, the people of the neighborhood protested and it was instead turned into a park.

Sylvia Rivera,
Trans Warrior

IN 1962,* eleven-year-old Ray Rivera appeared on the Forty-second Street hustling
scene in the once-glamorous theater district in
Midtown Manhattan. Described as "scrawny
but beautifully proportioned, with high, dra-
matic cheek bones and almond-shaped, lan-
guid eyes,"† he was quickly renamed Sylvia by
an older street queen trying to help him fit in to
the transvestite scene.

By 1969, having sworn off both hustling and
the heroin addiction that had dominated her
life for the previous half decade, Sylvia had settled into a comfortable relationship with a lover
named Gary. On the afternoon of June 27,
1969, having just heard of the death of the gay
icon Judy Garland, she warily agreed to a night
out at the Stonewall when her friend Tammy
Novak, a fellow transvestite notorious for her
drug use, called.

For the rest of the afternoon Sylvia
rethought her decision to meet her friend.
Though the Stonewall was known to be toler-
ant of men dressed as women, they weren't

particularly nice to them. And on nights when the bar was raided, police officers loved the opportunity to arrest men for violating a turn-of-the-century law prohibiting people from being in public wearing fewer than three articles of clothing that match their gender. (The law was originally written to protect landowners from harassment from tenant farmers who "donned disguises to demonstrate against their landlords"). But she had been saddened by Garland's death and thought a night out to mourn with her friends would do her good, so she and Gary went downtown with Tammy.

Sylvia and Gary were separated from Tammy after the raid and were waiting for her by the small park across the street from the bar after their IDs had been checked and they had been sent out. Sylvia spotted Tammy as she was being lined up with a number of other prisoners who were being loaded into the paddy wagon. The crowd began to chant Tammy's name, and Sylvia joined in with a shriek. Just then, a cop pushed Tammy and said, "Keep moving," as he began to tap her with his nightstick. Tammy told the cop to stop pushing, and when he didn't she started to swing at him.

When the cop began to fight back, Sylvia, according to many bystanders, threw the first Molotov cocktail at the riots. Moments later occurred the clubbing of the Stonewall Lesbian, which resulted in the igniting the full-scale rebellion.

Sylvia continued the fight for trans rights for years to come, founding an organization called STAR—Street Transvestite Action Revolutionaries. A section of Hudson Street beginning at its intersection of Christopher was named in honor of the trans hero. It is called Sylvia Rivera Way.

Q-Review

"Fat Tony" Lauria. Son of a high-ranking Mafioso, Ernie Lauria, "Fat Tony" Lauria bought the fire-gutted Stonewall Inn in the late 1960s and converted it into a bar catering to the gay community. Fat Tony and his associates were the main targets of the police raid on the Stonewall that culminated in the Stonewall Riots.

Seymour Pine. A decorated Vietnam veteran, in 1967 Pine was promoted from deputy inspector to head of the Brooklyn Police Department's Public Morals Division. Having had great success in Brooklyn, Pine was moved to Manhattan's First Division Morals, a more disorganized police unit, in the hopes that he would clean it up. Pine organized the raid on the Stonewall in June 1969 with the intention of shutting the establishment down for good. It was to be a first step in breaking the Mafia's control of all of the city's bars.

Craig Rodwell. Twenty-seven years old on the night he stumbled upon the Stonewall Riots, Rodwell, an ex-boyfriend of Harvey Milk's, was an aspiring activist. He is credited with throwing his fist in the air and screaming "Gay Power" while standing atop a stoop one door down from the Stonewall. "Gay Power!" became the battle cry of the riot and the liberation movement that followed. Rodwell would go on to organize the world's first gay pride march, the Christopher Street Liberation Day March, the following June. He is also the founder of the Oscar Wilde Memorial Bookshop, the nation's first all-gay bookstore.

The Stonewall Lesbian. She was the most intriguing attendee that night and her identity—even her existence—has been hotly debated. The beating by a police officer of a woman known as the Stonewall Lesbian is thought to have started the Stonewall Riot—but no one knew who this woman was. Now, for the first time since the riots, the "drag king" Storme DeLarverie has acknowledged that she was the Stonewall Lesbian. Nevertheless, some people believe that the Stonewall Lesbian was more than one person and others believe that she never existed at all and was invented in an attempt to further mythologize the riots and their significance.

Organizing

QUOTE

"There will be no heterosexual marriages today. It's gay day at the marriage bureau."

—Gay Activists' Alliance chant during "zap" of the New York City Marriage Bureau

IN LOOKING back over the days that followed the Stonewall Riots, it's clear that there was no one definitive response to the event. Many New Yorkers never heard anything about them, or if they did, it was from the brief snippets in the various newspapers that covered the fracas—most of whom covered the event as an attack on the police department and not as a homosexual uprising.

Within the gay community, reactions were divided as well. As in the wider community, there were those who heard of the event in passing and had no particular opinion. There were seasoned activists like Dick Leitsch, president of the Mattachine Society in New York, who were excited by the riots but nervous about making waves with the local authorities. And activism veterans like Randy Wicker (who has been called "the homophile movement's first East Coast militant")[*] feared that the riots would confirm society's every misconception as press coverage began to spread of "effeminate boys in the streets,[†] camping it up while drag queens joined gay men in a chorus line to kick their heels at cops and others set trash cans on fire."

And then of course there were the activists who saw the riots for what they were: a tipping point. As one historian, Tom Willenbecher, put it, "Stonewall happened along at the precise moment the movement was large enough to merit public attention and old enough to realize its own strength."[‡]

For those lesbians and gay men with foresight, anger, passion, and determination, the Stonewall Riots made one thing clear: it was time to shake things up. That meant rethinking and restructuring everything the community knew about organizing. Three organizations stand out among the many that were founded. Their legacies have withstood the test of time.

Gay Liberation Front (GLF)

The evening of June 29, 1969, was warm and balmy in New York City. Martha Shelley, an active member of New York's Daughters of Bilitis chapter who had recently stepped down as the organization's president, was showing a few of her DOB colleagues from Boston around the Village, when she noticed a raucous crowd near the Stonewall Inn. She ushered her guests away from the scene, explaining, "Oh [it's] just a riot. We have them here all the time."* Not until she read the paper the next afternoon did she realize that the riot she had stumbled upon was the second day of a homosexual revolt—the first scene of a revolt that would come to be known as the Stonewall Riots.

In an interview with the gay historian Michael Scherker, the first true historian of Stonewall, Shelley recalled her reaction to the discovery of the riot. "I was slightly feverish from lack of sleep, so I lay on my couch tossing and turning, so excited by it, thinking, 'We have to do something. We have to have a protest march.'"

Shelley and a number of others† took the idea of a march to Mattachine–New York and the Daughters of Bilitis—the only two of the seven or so gay organizations in the city who could reasonably pull off such an event. Dick Leitsch, agreed that something needed to be done, but had his sights set on holding a candlelight vigil in Washington Square Park. It would be a quiet and somber affair, one that was designed to avoid further angering city authorities. When put to a vote, the idea of a vigil was shot down by the more than 100 attendees of a Mattachine meeting held at Freedom House at 20 West Fortieth Street, in Midtown on July 9, 1969. The idea of a march won overwhelming support from the meeting participants, and those who volunteered to form a planning committee, headed by Martha Shelley, were told to move to a smaller room across the hall and start to get the idea together.

As soon as the activists were alone together, it was decided that the group needed a name. A number of unappealing ideas were put forward before someone, conjuring Vietnam's National Liberation Front—the Vietcong as they were known in the United States—suggested Gay Liberation Front. Shelley later recalled, "I started pounding on the table, saying, 'That's it! That's it! We're the gay liberation front.'"[*]

The group—which would be called the Mattachine Action Committee until a vote could be taken—immediately began working to plan for a rally and march, to be held on the one-month anniversary of the first Stonewall Riot, July 28. When the day came, roughly five hundred people showed up in Washington Square Park for the rally and then joined the march to the Stonewall Inn. The event went down in history as the first gay march in New York City, and credit for organizing and sponsoring it belonged to Mattachine–New York and the Daughters of Bilitis.

A few days later, on July 31, 1969, a meeting of the gay militants who had organized that march and others was held at Freedom House, a vote was taken, and the new group was officially christened the Gay Liberation Front. Splitting off from Mattachine, the group drafted a statement of purpose that read, "We are a revolutionary group of men and women formed with the realization that complete sexual liberation for all people cannot come about unless existing social institutions are abolished. We reject society's attempt to impose sexual roles and definitions of our nature."[†]

Though the group's loftier goals of "dismantling heterosexual marriage and the bourgeois family"[‡] sound almost alarmingly unrealistic, GLF is often credited with being the first organization to push the gay community to come out as a means of establishing themselves as a political force. They published a newspaper called *Come Out!* and encouraged gay people to be visible by bringing them together through dances and demonstrations. One of the first militant actions taken by GLF was the picketing of the *Village Voice* offices when the publication refused to allow the group to use the word "gay" in their advertisements. The *Voice* claimed to find the world "offensive."

The Gay Liberation Front's anti-assimilationist stance on activism and its ultrademocratic stance on governance, led to the speedy formation of chapters in a number of other cities around the United States and the United Kingdom, Canada, and Australia. Unfortunately, the elements that made the group successful in the beginning were ultimately its undoing in the end. GLF's ultrademocratic ideals and modus operandi are the reasons for it ultimate disintegration, according to the scholar Geoffrey W. Bateman: "Without formal leaders, members, or dues, the group, which operated by consensus, was radically democratic, sometimes chaotic, and often extremely divided on political issues." The lack of a firm central guiding entity led to the group's effectively disbanding in 1972.

Gay Activists Alliance (GAA)

It was a typical morning at the city clerk's office in downtown Manhattan that day in 1971.* Would-be newlyweds were expected throughout the day, as they were every day, to undertake the routine business of applying for marriage licenses. Business as usual, the clerk must have thought when he sat down at his desk that morning. That is, until he heard the ruckus in the hallway—the chanting, the yelling, the singing—and then heard a crack as his office door was forced open. All at once, the office was full of men and women, some in wedding gowns, some in tuxedos. A few in the group carried two different wedding cakes; at the top of one of them two plastic grooms stood kissing, at the top of the other, two plastic brides did the same. In a flurry of chanting and singing, a couple of people handcuffed themselves to desks while others picked up phones to alert the press. In a flash, an angry gentleman with shoulder-length brown hair, glasses, and a thick mustache stepped forward to speak for the group. He said, "There will be no heterosexual marriages today. It's gay day at the marriage bureau."* And with that, the Gay Activists Alliance, New York's newest and most active activist organization, shut down the city clerk's office, banning heterosexual marriage, if only for just a few short hours, as a means of protesting—or zapping, as the group called the tactic—the city's ban on gay marriage.

The Gay Activists Alliance was created in 1969 by four activists—Arthur Evans, Jim Owles, Marty Robinson, and Arthur Bell—in Bell's Greenwich Village apartment. Kay Tobin, the film historian Vito Russo, who later wrote *The Celluloid Closet*, and Morty Manford, whose parents were the future creators of PFLAG, are also credited with playing major roles in the creation of the organization.

Like many organizations, GAA was founded because of activists' frustrations with organizations already in place. Most all of GAA's founders were active members of Gay Liberation Front. They helped plan the marches and the protests. They attended the meetings and fundraisers. But they grew exhausted by the group's disorganization and frustrated by its cliques. They were unhappy with GLF's alliance with the Black Panthers—a group known for it's homophobic tendencies—and its sometimes non-gay-specific focuses like protesting the Vietnam War.

The handful of activists that gathered at Bell's apartment that night envisioned an organization with a single purpose: to secure basic human rights, dignity, and freedom for all gay people. In the minds of GAA's founders, they would achieve this by doing right all of the things GLF had done wrong.

Unlike GLF, whose ultrademocratic approach to running things often resulted in chaos and wasted time and energy, GAA felt that the best way to maximize its group's efforts was through organization and a strong sense of leadership. And so they drafted a constitution, elected officers, and established a system of committees in order to focus on issues that were of importance to a certain faction of the group. Committees with a focus on lesbian inclusion and black inclusion are two examples. GAA also opposed GLF's radical stance that gay equality would be won by overthrowing the system in order to rebuild it with a sense of gay inclusion. Instead, they sought to work within the system as out gay people. Although the group initially sought to attract people from all across the political spectrum by avoiding the endorsement of candidates for public office, the group did eventually get involved in the political process by "getting out the gay vote, running gay candidates, and working on behalf of gay-friendly candidates," as described in *Becoming Visible,* by Molly McGarry and Fred Wasserman.

Merle Miller, in *On Being Different* (1971), quotes a GAA cofounder, Arthur Bell: "Today we know not only that gay is good, gay is angry. We are telling all the politicians and elected officials of New York State that they are going to become responsible to the people. We will make them responsible to us, or we will stop the conduct of the business of government." Bell's threat was a real one.

Soon after the group's inception, GAA began staging political protests they called "zaps." Zaps, like the one held at the city clerk's office to protest the gay marriage ban, were meant to be grand and shocking, both as a way to seriously embarrass whoever or whatever was the target of the action and to garner media coverage. The first series of zaps staged by the group were directed at New York City Mayor John Lindsay. Though some in the gay community saw Lindsay as comparatively sympathetic to gays and lesbians, GAA took issue with his continuing to tolerate the raiding of gay bars and other forms of police harassment. GAA would zap Lindsay anywhere they could find him, whether at rallies he attended or, as with one famous example, in the lobby of the Metropolitan Opera House, where they shouted "Gay power!" and "End police harassment!" as he left the building.

Other well-known zaps, recounted by the gay historian Marc Rubin in his article "GAA Must Be Restored to History," include the takeover of the New York *Daily News* offices in response to a vicious antigay editorial; a sit-in in the offices of Governor Rockefeller as part of a push for the passage of a gay civil rights bill; a sit-in in the office of Gertrude Unser, president of the New York City Board of Education, to protest antigay bias in the hiring and firing of teachers and other staff; a protest at the headquarters of both ABC News and CBS News regarding the antigay tone of their reporting on issues touching the gay community. One result of these actions—but by no means the only one—was that ABC's notoriously antigay star, Dick Cavett, was forced to give airtime to GAA spokespeople on his nationally broadcast *Dick Cavett Show*.

Aside from the zaps, GAA was best known for the establishment of its headquarters in an abandoned firehouse at 99 Wooster Street, in SoHo. It was important to the group to maintain a focus on the establishment of the gay cultural movement that was gaining momentum alongside the political movement, which GAA was so involved in. And so the firehouse provided not only the comfort of a home base for the thriving organization but also a location where its members—and anyone else who chose to—could gather to celebrate all that was being accomplished.

Not since the establishment of the Oscar Wilde Memorial Bookshop had the gay community had a community center to call its own. The space provided by the firehouse was enormous in comparison to the meeting space offered by the bookshop—but it still wasn't always large enough to accommodate the thousands of people it drew to attend the wide variety of events held there, including discussion groups, self-defense classes, literary and theatrical events, and landmarks such as the first lesbian and gay film festival, organized by the gay film historian Vito Russo.

But perhaps the firehouse will best be remembered for the dances held there. A weekly tradition that began in May 1971, they were an immediate hit in the community. Some members of GAA feared that the popularity of the dances would distract the group from its commitment to the fight for gay equality. But it quickly became clear that the dances—attended by hundreds of people each week—provided GAA with a significant revenue stream while at the same time allowing the group to maintain the firehouse as an important meeting place and symbol of gay visibility.

With the passage of time since the days of the GAA dances, people who were there remember them differently. Some describe them as the gay community's first foray into multiculturalism, events where blacks, whites, women, and men were all well represented and all mixed it up and danced the night away with a sense of racially balanced brotherly and sisterly love. Others remember the dances as reflecting what was in fact the group's membership: predominantly white, middle-class men. Some women even cite the dances as providing them with the first visual image that accurately reflected the imbalance in the representation of women within the gay rights movement, an imbalance that had characterized the movement since its beginnings.

In October 1974 the firehouse was the target of arson—presumed to be one attack in a string of many aimed at gay establishments across the country at the time—and was burned beyond repair. The loss of its headquarters was a body blow to the fledgling organiza-

TIP

- According to the historian Marc Rubin, GAA was not mentioned in any of the press coverage or talked about during the reading of the timeline at the thirtieth-anniversary celebration of Stonewall in 1999. He fears that GAA "is being written out of history."
- The burning of the GAA firehouse was one in a string of anti-gay-related arsons. Others, as recounted in *Becoming Visible*, include two Metropolitian Community Churches (MCC is an association of churches that serve the GLBT community) in Los Angeles and San Francisco, and a gay bar in New Orleans, in which thirty-two people lost their lives. Gay bars in San Francisco and Springfield, Massachusetts, were attacked with fire bombs.
- In 1973, the National Gay and Lesbian Task Force, then named the National Gay Task Force, was founded by disgruntled members of GAA. It was the nation's first gay organization with a paid staff and a board of directors. NGLTF is still a vital organization in the fight for GLBT civil rights.

tion, which from that point forward suffered flagging membership and inefficient leadership. The group officially dissolved in 1981.

Lavender Menace

On the evening of May 1, 1970,* roughly three hundred women filed into the auditorium at Intermediate School 70 on West Seventeenth Street in Manhattan. They were members of the feminist organization, the National Organization of Women (NOW), which was holding its Second National Congress to Unite Women. As the first scheduled speaker approached the microphone, the auditorium went dark and the sound system was disabled. A full-on GAA-style "zap" was under way. Karla Jay, an activist who helped plan the zap, explains what came next in her book *Tales of the Lavender Menace:*

> I was planted in the middle of the audience, and I could hear my coconspirators running down both aisles. Some were laughing while others were emitting rebel yells. When [activists] Michaela [Griffo] and Jesse [Falstein] flipped the lights back on, both aisles were lined with seventeen lesbians wearing their Lavender Menace T-shirts and holding the placards we had made. Some invited the audience to join them. I stood up and yelled, "Yes, yes, sisters! I'm tired of being in the closet because of the women's movement." Much to the horror of the audience, I unbuttoned the long-sleeved red blouse I was wearing and ripped it off. Underneath, I was wearing a Lavender Menace T-shirt. There were

hoots of laughter as I joined the others in the aisles. Then Rita [Mae Brown] yelled to members of the audience, "Who wants to join us?"

"I do, I do," several replied.

Then Rita also pulled off her Lavender Menace T-shirt. Again, there were gasps, but underneath she had on another one. More laughter. The audience was on our side.

The zap by the group of lesbians had been Rita Mae Brown's idea. Brown, who would go on to be the best-selling author of such books as *Rubyfruit Jungle*, had been active in the civil rights movement, the antiwar movement, and the gay rights movement in the late 1960s before taking an administrative job with NOW. Like many lesbians of the day, she felt her energy was best spent working for lesbian equality within the women's movement rather than with groups such as GLF or GAA, which placed a much higher emphasis on advancing the rights of gay men than those of gay women. Although feminist groups such as NOW often seemed less than passionate about the struggle for lesbian equality, it came as a shock when in 1969 Betty Friedan, NOW's president, publicly referred to lesbians as a "lavender menace" to the feminist movement. She feared that an association with lesbians would hamper the group's ability to effect real political change and would leave the group open to stereotypical charges of man hating. The organization had dropped the New York chapter of Daughters of Bilitis from its list of sponsors for its First National Congress to Unite Women, in November 1969.

Freidan's actions so outraged—and personally of-fended—Brown that she resigned her position with NOW and suggested to other lesbians that they organize and take action. Putting a spin on Friedan's putdown, the group adopted Lavender Menace as their name, and the zap became their coming-out party.

In addition to storming the stage that night, the group placed on every seat in the auditorium a ten-paragraph manifesto bearing the title "The Woman-Identified Woman," which challenged all feminists to reconsider their preconcieved ideas of lesbians and lesbianism. It opens with the following challenge:

> What is a lesbian? A lesbian is the rage of all women condensed to the point of explosion. She is the woman who, often beginning at an extremely early age, acts in accordance with her inner compulsion to be a more complete and freer human being than her society—perhaps then, but certainly later—cares to allow her. These needs and actions, over a period of years, bring her into painful conflict with people, situations, the accepted ways of thinking, feeling and behaving, until she is in a state of con-tinual war with everything around her, and usually with her self.

Kate Millett, chairwoman of NOW at the time of the Second National Congress to Unite Women, had been alerted to Lavender Menace's plan. She encouraged the group to stage their protest and also encouraged the au-dience to listen to what the women had to say. According to Jay's account, it didn't take long to win the crowd over. When a few members of the planning committee tried to take the stage back from the women, the audience booed the action and applauded the Menaces to continue. With that show of support, the Menaces embarked on what became, according to most accounts, a two-hour open-mike-style discussion of lesbianism in the feminist movement.

The zap was so successful that many of the members of Lavender Menace were asked to lead impromptu seminars and workshops on lesbianism and homophobia throughout the weekend. An all-women dance was put together to celebrate the group's accomplishment and was attended by both gay and straight women. And, perhaps most important, at the congress's final assembly, a number of pro-lesbian resolutions were proposed by the group and adopted by NOW.

Following their success with the NOW congress, the group changed its name to Lesbian Liberation, before ultimately becoming Radicalesbians. It was an organization that prided itself on having a nonhierarchical structure—similar to the Gay Liberation Front's—and making decisions by consensus. The historian Linda Rapp, writing for GLBTQ.com, stated: "The Radicalesbians believed in absolute female separatism and refused to associate with men or with women who did not cut their ties to mainstream heterosexual society. They even denounced their recent ally Millett as a 'collaborator.'" This belief system, along with their disorganized approach to governance, was ultimately the group's undoing. Suffering from flagging membership, the group disbanded in early 1972.

The Christopher Street Liberation Day March

On the morning of Sunday, June 28, 1970,* thirty-year-old Craig Rodwell paced nervously around his small apartment on Bleecker Street. The sun was shining and there was not a cloud in the sky. There was even a bit of a chill in the air, which meant that by noon the temperature would be comfortable—a perfect day to carry off his plan. All he was waiting for now was the knock at his door—it would be a police officer from the Sixth Precinct, delivering the permit for the march he and his cohorts on the planning committee had spent the previous year putting together. It had taken six meetings with the police department for the permit to be promised, and now, as the minutes ticked away before the planned start of the event, Rodwell made a decision: the march was going to take place, permit or no permit. Just as he was about to give up and leave, the knock came and an officer handed over the permit.

The idea for the march had come to Rodwell a year before. It was July 4, 1969—just six days after the Stonewall Riots—that he and a group of other New York activists, including Barbara Gittings, were on a chartered bus to Philadelphia. It was the fifth year in a row that the group had made the trip on that day to hold a demonstration they called the "Annual Reminder" in front of Independence Hall. The demonstration consisted of twelve to twenty people who were formally dressed and held signs that read "Homosexuals Are Citizens Too" and other equally unoffensive slogans as they marched in a circle in front of the building.

That year, Rodwell was pumped, still riding the high of the take-no-prisoners and make-no-apologies riots he had stumbled upon at the Stonewall less than a week before. "The night of the Stonewall Riots," he would tell the historian Martin Duberman years later, "I was walking home and I saw the crowd in Sheridan Square. I turned to my friend and said, 'This is it. That crowd is the spark that could turn this into a mass movement.'"* A few minutes after making that statement, Rodwell climbed the seven steps of the stoop next-door to the Stonewall, threw his fist in the air, and yelled "Gay power!" The phrase was immediately adopted as the slogan for the early years of the gay civil rights movement.

Determined not to lose the momentum gained by the burgeoning movement that night, Rodwell worked practically around the clock in the days that followed the riots. A few years before he had founded a small activist group called the Homophile Youth Movement in Neighborhoods (HYMN), so he knew that the only way to carry off his mission was to get the community organized. First he put together a leaflet outlining what had taken place that fateful night, what the political ramifications were, and how gay and lesbian people could best use the events of June 29, 1969, to their advantage. He then spent days distributing the flyer up and down Christopher Street and around Sheridan Square. But it didn't seem like enough to him, and still he feared that eventually the excitement generated by the Stonewall Riots would die down, people would forget, and all that had been gained would be lost.

And then, on the bus to Philadelphia, he had an epiphany: A year to the day after the riots at Stonewall, the gay and lesbian community would hold the first annual march to commemorate the event. "I was always so afraid the movement was going to die out," he told Duberman. "So we have to have an annual event as a constant reminder."* And he gave the march the perfect name: the Christopher Street Liberation Day March.

Rodwell got to work immediately. First he assembled a committee of other activists who shared his commitment to keeping the Stonewall Riots relevant. Next, the committee sent notices out to the other prominent gay and lesbian organizations asking for man- and womanpower and money in order to get the idea off the ground. GLF responded to the call immediately, supplying the committee with tireless and enthusiastic volunteers. GAA followed suit, but not until about two months before the march. Noticeably absent from the planning was the Mattachine Society of New York, the city's oldest gay organization, which by then had issued a statement declaring that its members were against the idea. Also absent was Daughters of Bilitis, the city's sole lesbian organization. Many in the New York chapter of DOB shared the belief of their national president, Shirley Weller, who in 1966 had declared that "demonstrations which define the homosexual as a unique minority defeat the very cause for which the homosexual strives—to be an integral part of society."† At the last minute, though, with just weeks to go before the event, both groups changed their positions and became involved.‡

Despite the number of volunteers and the general excitement that was growing among the committee members, fundraising had been a problem from the beginning. Foster Gunnison, the committee's treasurer and secretary, according to Duberman's history, "sent out notices to all East Coast Homophile Organizations asking for $10 donations." He also sent pleading letters of appeal, written on Oscar Wilde Memorial Bookshop letterhead, to various individuals, which read:

GAY PRIDE WEEK, JUNE 22–28[*]
June 22nd through June 28, 1970, has been designated GAY PRIDE WEEK by the Christopher Street Liberation Day Committee. The CSLDC is a coalition effort by most of the homophile organizations on the East Coast.

While many of the area homophile organizations will be holding separate observances during GAY PRIDE WEEK (dances, discussions, leafleting, etc.), the focus of the Christopher Street Liberation Day Committee is the planning of a mass march from the Christopher Street area in Greenwich Village through midtown Manhattan on Sixth Avenue to the Sheep Meadow in Central Park for a "Gay-In." Assembly time for the march is 1 PM and the march will start at 2 PM on Sunday, June 28th.

Needless to say, a lot of money is needed to advertise and plan the march and the "Gay-In." We of the Homophile Youth Movement (HYMN) strongly urge you to support GAY PRIDE WEEK and CHRISTOPHER STREET LIBERATION DAY (June 28th). And we hope you will want to join the thousands of proud homosexual men and women in peacefully observing GAY PRIDE WEEK and by marching in the mass march on CHRISTOPHER STREET LIBERATION DAY, Sunday, June 28th.

The success of GAY PRIDE WEEK and the mass march on CHRISTOPHER STREET LIBERATION DAY will be determined not only by the numbers of people participating but by the amount of funds and help available for advertising and planning. With this in mind, the Homophile Youth Movement (HYMN) and the Oscar Wilde Memorial Bookshop urge you to contribute your time and/or money to the Christopher Street Liberation Day Committee by filling out the coupon below and sending it in. (A full accounting of the Committee's expenses will be sent to all contributors.)

The financial turnout was significantly less impressive than the committee had hoped. It quickly became clear that the two-day block party they had wanted to precede the event was out of the question, as the city of New York at that time required a bond of $1 million to protect against damage. They were, however, able to raise just over $1,100, with which they were able to put on the march that year.

The next problem was guaranteeing turnout. The committee was smart to plan the march for Sunday the twenty-eighth, which was technically the day *after* the one-year anniversary of the Stonewall Riots. Rodwell's explanation for that was "more people would be free to participate on a Sunday and it would be easier to obtain permits and in general cut through the red tape"* than on any other day of the week. And then there was the issue of making people feel safe. Essentially, partici-

TIP

One crimson armband from the first Christopher Street Liberation Day March bearing the initials CSLDM written on it in black Magic Marker has survived. It was donated to the New York Public Library by Craig Rodwell as part of the collection of papers he donated to the archives and manuscripts division.

pating in the march was publicly coming out. In 1970 that was an incredibly risky business for most people. In an effort to reassure potential participants, flyers advertising the march were created using pictures of people where one could *actually see* people's faces. It was the first time in the history of the movement in New York City that people allowed their likenesses to be used in connection with a gay event. Also, Foster Gunnison recruited and trained peacekeepers and marshals—they wore crimson armbands—to be on hand the entire time to answer any questions and provide assistance to marchers in need.

The march Rodwell planned was quite long, and he did this on purpose. The march was to start at Sheridan Square—near Sixth Avenue and Waverly Place—and proceed up Sixth Avenue to Central Park, where a rally, the Gay-In, was to be held on the Sheep Meadow. His hope was that the organizations involved with the committee and the street youths who felt they had nothing to lose would start the march off strong and that others would join in once they saw that everything was safe.

Rodwell got down to the assembly point a little after noon. He was wearing a striped button-down collared shirt and a pair of slacks—and, as the day began to heat up, was especially grateful that Mattachine Society–enforced coats and ties at such demonstrations had become a thing of the past. Permit in hand, he had a brief conversation with some of the police officers who had been assigned to the event. He would recall later that there were "lots of them" and that most appeared "indifferent." According to Duberman's account, "No more than a handful of cops seemed openly hostile."

Copies of a flyer Rodwell had written were being distributed to members of the gathering crowd. It read:

Welcome

Welcome to the first anniversary* of the gay liberation movement. We are united today to affirm our pride, our lifestyle, and our commitment to each other. Despite political and social differences we may have, we are united on this common ground: For the first time in history we are together as the Homosexual Community. This is the commitment that draws us together; let us not forget it throughout this, our day.

Placing this commitment above all else, let nothing stand in our way. We are gay and proud. No one can convince us otherwise. Degrading remarks by hecklers or observers are not important enough to interfere with our goal and don't deserve a reaction.

The Christopher Street Liberation Day Committee has worked closely with the New York City Police Dept. and we have received their full cooperation to insure an orderly and successful march. Trained marshals are marked with orange CSLD armbands; they are members of the Gay Community and are here to serve the people by providing important information such as medical and legal aid, parade routes, and the location of rest areas. Feel free to ask them any and all questions; they are here to help you in every way possible.

Everyone of us is important. We are showing our strength and love for each other by coming here today. We are all participants in the most important gay event in history.

The Christopher Street
Liberation Day Committee

Looking around at the gathering crowd, Rodwell tried to count the number of people who would be joining him and the rest of the committee when the march kicked off at 2 P.M. He gave up when it became impossible to discern the definite marchers from those who'd shown up to watch—undecided as to whether they would participate. Frustrated, he began to pace up and down Waverly Place, estimating that less than a thousand people would be brave enough to march with him.

The official start of the march was delayed for fifteen minutes in hopes that more people would show up and

TIP

The 1970 Christopher Street Liberation Day March was the first and only time the march route was from the West Village north to Central Park. Starting in 1971, the march followed the route in the opposite direction so as to bring business to the gay-owned and -operated establishments of the West Village.

that some of the undecideds would find the courage to participate. Then, at 2:15, the kick-off signal was given and the march began to move. Foster Gunnison would recall in his interview with Duberman that "everyone was scared to death." For that reason, the march moved quickly up Sixth Avenue. As it progressed, it grew in size, and the number of participants doubled before the marchers reached the halfway point.

According to Duberman's history, there were few hecklers: "Aside from a few predictable (19A)Sodom and Gomorrah signs, and a Black Panther newspapers hawker shouting, 'Get the Panther paper and stop all this foolishness!' the reaction of the spectators ranged from frozen to benign to overtly encouraging. The only persistent pests were tourists snapping photographs."

TIP The Christopher Street Liberation Day Committee, under different leadership each year, organized the march and rally until 1994 when Heritage of Pride was created. Heritage of Pride has organized the events every year since and has added their own annual events which include: Rapture of the River, a boat cruise for lesbians; Pridefest, a street festival; and the Peer Dance on Pier 20.

The march reached Central Park in a little over an hour. By then the estimated number participants ranged from 5,000 to 10,000 (and in one case up to 20,000—a number that was obviously inflated). Thanks to Rodwell's and the rest of the committee's efforts, the Christopher Street Liberation Day March had incarnations in other cities that day. Of course, New York's demonstration was by far the largest—more than three times the numbers of marchers in any other city. Rodwell was elated that his idea had come to fruition in such grand fashion. And he couldn't have imagined that the demonstration he had conceived of—one held as a show of defiance and courage—would become the international celebration future generations would call Pride.

The march was covered by most major newspapers. The *New York Times*—which had given scant coverage to the Stonewall Riots—ran the story of the march on the front page.

Parents and Friends of Lesbians and Gays (PFLAG)

On the night of June 28, 1969,* nineteen-year-old Morty Manford was at his favorite bar, the Stonewall Inn. "The Stonewall was my favorite place," he recalled years later to the historian Eric Marcus for his book *Making History*. "It was a dive. It was shabby, and the glasses they served the watered-down drinks in weren't particularly clean." He describes noticing a few men in suits and ties entering the bar and walking around a bit as whispers began to circulate that the place was being raided. When the lights came up and everyone was told to show the police their identification and then leave, Manford was one of the hundreds that gathered outside the bar and ultimately participated in the riot. Despite the fact that his life "pretty much revolved around going to the bars," it was the only bar raid he ever experienced.

The Stonewall Riot was a turning point in Manford's life. He was a student at Columbia University, where the Student Homophile League was the first gay student group to be officially recognized by a college or university. He had joined the group with the hope of getting involved with the burgeoning gay rights movement but had given up attending meetings because of the group's lack of organization and action. The Stonewall Riot and his subsequent involvement with GLF changed his attitude that the gay liberation movement was at a standstill.

After attending the fifth annual Philadelphia reminder—a protest held annually on July 4 to "remind" the world of homosexual inequality—with Barbara Gittings and Craig Rodwell (on the very trip during which Rodwell conceived of the Christopher Street Liberation Day March), Manford joined Gay Activists Alliance. He immediately became an integral force behind the group's zaps. Protesting, it seemed, was in his blood.

Another turning point in Manford's life came during a GAA protest near the New York City Hilton Hotel, when he was brutally beaten—punched in the face, kicked repeatedly, and then thrown down an escalator— by an antigay attendee. The police reportedly watched the attack and did nothing to stop it.

Manford's parents, Jeanne and Jules Manford, heard about the attack on their son that day, and they watched images of further brutality at the Hilton protest on the television news that evening. In an article written by journalist Tom Owens, Manford's parents said they were "outraged that the police appeared to ignore the assault."

The following day, when there was no mention of the event in the *New York Times*, Mrs. Manford called the paper's editorial offices to find out why. She says she was hung up on. In fact, of all of the city's major newspapers, only the *New York Post* ran significant coverage of the protest and the fact that police officers turned a blind eye to the beatings. Mrs. Manford wrote the *Post*'s editors to commend them on the story. Published in the April 29, 1972, edition, the letter read:

I would like to commend The Post for its coverage last week of the tragic incident that took place at the Inner Circle Dinner, when hoodlums who work for our city were allowed to beat up the young men of the Gay Activists Alliance and walk away while our police stood by watching. It might be that these "men" themselves have some deep rooted sexual problems or they would not have become so enraged as to commit violence in beatings.

I am proud of my son Morty Manford and the hard work he has been doing in urging homosexuals to accept their feelings and not let bigots and sick people take advantage of them in the ways they have done in the past and are continuing to do.

I hope that your honest and forthright coverage of the incident has made many of the gays who have been fearful gain courage to come out and join the bandwagon. They are working for a fair chance at employment and dignity and to become a vocal and respected minority. It is a fight for recognition such as all minority groups must wage and needs support from outsiders as well as participants in the movements.

—Jeanne Manford

It was a groundbreaking moment, but as Mrs. Manford now says, "I didn't think anything of it, but I guess it was the first time a mother ever [publicly] said, 'Yes, I have a homosexual child.'"

Morty had had a difficult time believing that his parents—his mother especially—could be so excepting of his homosexuality. "Of course, I knew Morty was gay," his mother told Tom Owens. "He didn't want to tell me. I told him that I loved him, and nothing else mattered. At first there was a little tension there. He didn't believe I was that accepting." But the letter in the *Post* changed his mind. He called his mother the next day to tell her how grateful he was. In the months that followed the publication of her letter, she was invited on the *Phil Donahue Show* as well as a number of other television programs whose hosts and producers were interested in having discussions with parents of gay children. Two months later, in June of 1972, Morty invited his mother to walk with him in the second annual Christopher Street Liberation Day Parade. She was thrilled at the invitation and made a large poster board sign that read "Parents of Gays Unite in Support of Our Children."

The day of the parade was warm. Morty wore a pair of jeans, a white button-down shirt, and a sport coat. His mother wore a knee-length skirt and a pair of boots. She had brought a coat with her that she didn't need and so draped it over one arm while holding the sign she had made as high as she could with her free hand. As the march kicked off and the Manfords began their walk down Fifth Avenue, they were greeted at every block with an overwhelming volume of cheers. At first they thought the outpouring was for Dr. Benjamin Spock, the famed author of the book *Baby and Child Care*, who also was participating in the march. But as parade watchers ran into the street in droves to speak to Mrs. Manford— hug her, ask her to speak to their parents—it quickly became clear that the cheering was for them.

"As we marched the parade route," Mrs. Manford remembered years later, Morty and I began talking about starting a group for parents... I remember as we marched telling Morty that I hoped it would someday become a national organization, but that was just a dream. I never envisioned we would reach so many people."

Creating the national organization that would come to be known as PFLAG (Parents and Friends of Lesbians and Gays) started slowly. Initially it was just Mrs. Manford fielding hundreds of calls a week from gays and lesbians as well as their parents all around the country who had heard of her and wanted advice. When it became clear that there was enough of a need, Mrs. Manford put together the group's first official meeting. It was held at the Metropolitan Duane Methodist Church in Greenwich Village. Approximately twenty people attended.

Since the initial meeting where parents gathered to share their stories and try to understand how to best support their children, the organization has grown exponentially. In 1974, Larry and Adele Starr formed the Los Angeles group and became the first parents' group to apply for nonprofit, tax-exempt status. In 1979 the group from both coasts organized a contingent of marchers for the first national march for gay and lesbian rights in Washington, DC. And then, amid the obvious need for local chapters across the country, more than thirty people met at the Starrs' home in Los Angeles to write the bylaws for a national organization, give it a name, and draft the articles of incorporation. "We sent out for food, had pizza and drank beer," Mrs. Starr would recall later. "We really spent forty-eight hours together and formed the national organization."

TIP Morty Manford went on to become an assistant district attorney for the state of New York. He died of AIDS-related complications in 1992.

PFLAG now has over 200,000 members and supporters and over 500 affiliates in the United States. The poster that Jeanne Manford proudly carried as she marched in 1972 is a part of the International Gay Information Center collection at the New York Public Library.

Q-Review

Martha Shelley. One of the major forces behind the creation of both the Gay Liberation Front and Lavender Menace. Shelley was also one of the brainchildren behind the first march to commemorate the riot at Stonewall, which took place one month to the day after the event.

Arthur Bell. Founding member of the Gay Activists Alliance and author of *Dancing the Gay Lib Blues: A Year in the Homosexual Liberation Movement* (1972). Among other things, he is remembered for publicly putting the government of New York City on notice that they would become responsible to gay and lesbian people or the gay community would "stop the conduct of business."

Vito Russo. Founding member of the Gay Activists Alliance, a noted journalist and film historian, and the author of T*he Celluloid Closet*. He served as a consultant for *Common Threads—Stories from the Quilt*, and the Academy Award–winning documentary *The Times of Harvey Milk*.

Betty Friedan. Pioneer feminist whose best-selling book, *The Feminine Mystique*, is often credited with serving as the catalyst for the nation's second wave of feminism. She recanted the antilesbian stance she took early in her career by later stating that she had been "very square" and "was uncomfortable with homosexuality." At a women's conference in Houston in 1977, held to ratify the United Nations "Platform for Women," she seconded a motion supporting lesbian rights.

Rita Mae Brown. Early civil rights activist whose notion that lesbians should take action in response to Betty Friedan's homophobic comment resulted in the creation of the group Lavender Menace. She is the author of best-selling lesbian classics such as *Rubyfruit Jungle* and *Venus Envy*.

Artemis March. Credited with being the "chief author" of the Lavender Menace's manifesto, "The Woman-Identified Woman." The document is considered to be one of the most important writings of the early years of the gay rights movement. At the time the document was written, March was known as March Hoffman.

Foster Gunnison. An important early LGBT activist throughout the late 1960s and '70s. He was an integral part of the planning of the first Christopher Street Liberation Day March; he was in charge of fundraising, accounting, and recruiting and training parade marshals. His meticulous financial records for the march were kept by Craig Rodwell and are included in the collection of papers Rodwell donated to the New York Public Library.

Shirley Weller. President of the New York Chapter of Daughters of Bilitis at the time of the first Christopher Street Liberation Day March, she encouraged the group's members to not participate out of fear that the march would further marginalize the lesbian and gay community.

Brenda Howard. Describes herself as a bisexual, "sex-positive" feminist activist. Involved with the gay rights movement before and after Stonewall, Howard came up with the idea of having a number of events take place surrounding the Christopher Street Liberation Day March. Her idea was adopted—and is still used—by most Gay Pride planning committees around the world. Just before her death in 2005, she was quoted in a gay publication as saying, "Next time someone asks you why LGBT Pride marches exist or why Gay Pride Month is June, tell them, 'A bisexual woman named Brenda Howard thought it should be.'"

Jeanne Manford. Cofounder of the organization that became Parents and Friends of Lesbians and Gays (PFLAG).

CHAPTER FOUR

Our Sexual Revolution

QUOTE

> "There is a palpable sense of adventure or danger, but either way, something is about to happen."

BY THE EARLY 1970s, as activist groups continued to spring up and the gay community continued to get better at organizing and fighting for its rights, the political movement was well under way in New York City. But there was another movement afoot—a movement that would be remembered more as a revolution: sexual liberation.

Coming out of the 1960s free-love era, 1970s New York City fostered the idea of sexual exploration and self-identification. And for the first time in history, gay men were able to rid themselves of the shame they had been raised with and embark on the journey of sexual self-discovery. It is a time that the filmmaker Joseph Lovett has called "the most libertine period the western world has ever seen since Rome." His film *Gay Sex in the*

70s explores the hows and wheres of the revolution that would change the course of gay history.

Christopher Street

Originally a rural path called Skinner Road in seventeenth-century New Amsterdam, the street was officially paved and christened Christopher when the land it was on was purchased by Charles Christopher Amos in 1799.

Christopher Street, almost from its beginnings, was never a stranger to drama. As the street developed throughout the 1800s and attracted artists and other "creative types" to what was quickly becoming a downtown bohemia, tensions arose between the working-class residents at the western end and the artistic set who had settled on the eastern end. These class riots developed into a sort of race war by the 1930s. Wayne Hoffman, in an article he wrote for the *Village Voice,* described how "race riots erupted in 1932 between striking white longshoremen and black strikebreakers. Social tensions among different ethnic communities often led to street fights."

Gays and lesbians had long been a part of the scene on Christopher Street, but it wasn't until around this period, the1930s, that the group was able to be publicly identified. Even then, they were acknowledged only as a draw to the Village, the way sideshow freaks were a draw to a carnival. In his book *Gay New York, 1890–1940*, the historian George Chauncey describes the time period:

> The history of two cafeterias in the Village in the 1920s and 1930s, Stewart's and the Life Cafeteria, both located on Christopher Street at Sheridan

Square, demonstrated even more clearly the extent to which gay men could be made part of the spectacle of an establishment, even as they turned it into a haven. Both cafeterias…seemed to have premised their late night operations on the assumption that by allowing lesbians and gay men to gather there they would attract sight-seers out to gawk at the late-night "fairy hangout."

Chauncey goes on to explain that although the lesbians and gay men may have felt a bit objectified, it was a small price to pay for finding a place where the owner allowed them to gather and more or less be themselves. "Although gay men served as a tourist attraction* at the Life, they were still able to make it their own, turning it into one of the few places where their culture predominated and where they could anticipate meeting their friends."

As time went on and the shipping industry, which dominated Christopher Street for the first half of the twentieth century, declined, many of the local establishments that catered almost exclusively to maritime workers were left in need of a new clientele. "Many of those places† that had been seamen's bars and longshoremen's bars became gay bars," Alan Berbue, an urban historian, recalled.

The real increase in gay visibility on Christopher Street occurred in the 1960s, as new gay bars continued to pop up on the street. With the piers and trucks on the West Side Highway, there was a constant stream of gay traffic on Christopher Street in order to get to them. Many remember that era as the freest and most open time for gay men up to that point, but the new visibility came with a price. Gay men and lesbians suffered constant brutal violence at the hands of both gay bashers and the police.

With the Stonewall Riots in June of 1969, everything changed for gay and lesbian people everywhere, but especially and most dramatically for those who lived and played around Stonewall's Ground Zero: Christopher Street. Bob Kohler, a longtime Village resident who was at Stonewall on the night of the raid, recalled to Hoffman that Christopher Street that summer—where, in the wake of the riot, there was a police presence twenty-four/seven— "looked like an armed camp. Everybody was waiting for the next riot." Of course, instead of continuing to riot, the gay community organized, and "within weeks," Hoffman wrote, "Gay Liberation Front formed and organized a peaceful 'stoop-in,' in which gay people sat on stoops to claim Christopher Street sidewalks as 'gay turf.'"

Christopher Street thrived throughout the 1970s, but in the early 1980s things took a terrible turn. The wonderful freedom of sexual liberation led to the devastating epidemic that was AIDS. As Village residents died by the thousands, Christopher Street suffered the worst economic, spiritual, and social blows imaginable. With such an enormous loss of the gay and lesbian clientele that had kept the business on Christopher Street vital and thriving for decades, more and more restaurants and shops were forced to close every day.

But the spirit of Christopher Street could not be broken. And even as the young and hip discovered the trendier neighborhoods of Chelsea and Hell's Kitchen

In May of 2006,* city officials announced a new historic district called the Weehawken Street Historic District. The district starts at the corner of Christopher and Weehawken streets and ends slightly beyond West Tenth Street. It was marked a historic district because, according to the preservation society, it is "chock full of references to the area's gay history" and was "critical to gay life after the Stonewall Rebellion."

and these areas, too, exploded with gay bars, coffee shops, and restaurants, Christopher Street lived on in reverie as the city's oldest gay landmark. Today, Christopher Street mainstays such as the Oscar Wilde Memorial Bookshop, the Stonewall Inn, the Duplex, Ty's, and the Factory coffee shop thrive. And despite the sudden appearance of national chain establishments, Christopher Street remains the best place in New York to see Pride flags dangling from apartment windows, a good old leather shop, or a couple of guys holding hands as they stroll down the street.

The Piers

By the mid-1950s, the shipping industry,* which had dominated New York City's Hudson River waterfront since the early 1800s, was in serious decline. One by one the piers that skirt the West Village section of the West Side Highway were abandoned. The docks and the buildings that surrounded them—places that had bustled with ferries, ocean liners, passengers, and cargo for more than a century and a half—were suddenly empty. The historian Alan Berbue once said, "The piers, as they became vacant and decayed, became kind of an urban wilderness."

By the mid-1970s, Christopher Street was acting as a huge magnet for the whole gay community in New York City—it was packed with crowds of people—and it didn't take long for a handful of guys to find and take advantage of the solitude offered in the piers' vacated buildings. The piers are described by some who discovered them early on as a beautiful location that was quiet and good for sunbathing. Right from the beginning, the gay men who hung out on the piers knew it was a place they could be free with themselves. In pictures from that time, men can be seen walking the piers in jockstraps, underwear, or nothing at all. Word of the piers spread quickly among the men who frequented Christopher Street and the piers soon became the city's best-known cruising spot for gay men.

While the pier was heavily cruised during daylight hours, it was also a bit of a social scene as day workers from local meat-packing plants came to sit on the docks and enjoy the afternoon sun on their lunch breaks. According to the men who cruised the piers during that time, it was at night that all the boys came out. Roger McFarlane, an activist and writer, said in an interview that appeared in Joseph Lovett's film *Gay Sex in the 70s*, "There were thousands of people fucking in the dark. Every day of the week. No matter what the weather."

Being old and decrepit, the abandoned buildings on the piers were never maintained or inspected by the city, so the men who cruised there were taking their lives into their own hands every time they entered these old hulks. It was not unusual for a man either to fall through a whole in the floor or simply to crash through the rotted wood he was standing on and plunge into the Hudson River. On more than a handful of occasions, officers from the Sixth Precinct were called in to pull a floating corpse out of the water.

As they did with all known cruising spots, the police patrolled the piers and arrested those they caught. Eventually most of the buildings on the piers were torn down, and then most of the piers themselves were torn down; but the Christopher Street Pier was beautifully renovated by the city's parks department in 2003.

The Trucks

David Carter explains in *Stonewall: The Riots That Sparked the Gay Revolution*, "Commercial trucks that hauled* produce and other cargo into the city usually unloaded their goods either at warehouses or waterfront loading docks. While the trucks were waiting for a load to take back out of the city, the empty trucks were parked unattended, with the backs unlocked." Gay men adopted the waterfront trucks as a cruising spot and they became so popular that, according to one unnamed village resident, "What made Christopher Street so gay* was the fact that the trucks were at the end of it."

There is a beautiful black and white picture by the photographer Alvin Baltrop of the trucks at the height of their popularity in the 1970s. Taken from the north, the picture shows a view of the southern portion of Manhattan at midnight. Small fluorescent lights dot the elevated section of the West Side Highway, where the trucks are parked below. The dirty and travel-worn vehicles rest under the watchful eyes of the looming twin towers. The streets are vacant, but one gets the sense that people are watching and waiting just outside the frame. There is a palpable sense of adventure or danger, but either way something is about to happen.

Hundreds—and by some accounts thousands—of men made their way to the trucks each night. Some cruised the loading docks and the small alleys in between. Others were couples with no place else to go. They all made their way into the dark abysses where they knew to watch their wallets in pursuit of the sexual encounters they had come there for.

Despite the fact that the trucks grew so popular that eventually a street vendor took up residence there—he sold everything from water and soda to lubricant—not everyone loved the trucks. Surely with the stale smell of sweat, sex, and poppers they were not for the sexually conservative. In addition, however, the danger—of group arrests by homophobic police as well as from rumored pickpockets and potential gay bashers lurking in the dark—were enough to keep many people away.

Its important to note that sex at the piers and in the trucks wasn't just about recreation; it was also a product of the homophobic practices of the time, which often left gay people with no other options. "If we had our druthers,"* one gay man, Marle Becker, told Carter, "we would have been happier checking into a hotel like any other couple, but that wasn't always an option for us." Remembering how he and his lover had been turned away from a hotel because they were gay, he continued, "There wasn't anyplace for us to go. If you didn't have an apartment or you had roommates or what have you [the only option] was to have sex in Central Park or the trucks or some out-of-the-way place where hopefully you didn't get caught and arrested."

The Bars

In the post-Stonewall 1970s, the Mafia slowly began to lose their grip on gay bars in New York City. In popular gay neighborhoods all over town new bars catering to the various segments of the gay population seemed to pop up daily. On the Upper West Side—where Central Park West had long been a popular cruising spot (due largely to its proximity to the Rambles, a highly wooded area of Central Park popular with gay men as a place to have sex)—gay bars lined the avenues and streets. Wildwood, Warehouse, Boot Hill, and The Works are a few of the Upper West Side gay bars that opened during that time, but The Works was the only bar with any real staying power. The establishment became a sort of unofficial neighborhood landmark and remained open from the early 1970s until 2003, when it was gutted and turned into a hair salon.

The 1970s also brought gay culture to Chelsea, the West Side neighborhood just north of Fourteenth Street. Up to that point, wrote Michael Shernoff in a 1997 article in *LGNY*, a gay New York City–based newspaper, it was "a drab and gritty working-class neighborhood, populated by a combination of Irish, often the descendants of longshoremen who worked the Chelsea docks, Latinos, a sprinkling of upper-middle-class, and some pockets of gay men."* But as gays and lesbians moved to New York in droves and housing in the Village was both nearly impossible to find and increasingly expensive, Chelsea became the place where many people settled. And it didn't take long for bar and club owners to capitalize on the neighborhood's new residents. Shernoff describes how new bars seemed to appear overnight— places such as "The Eagle, The Spike, The Ramp† (on West Street), and even the first gay dance bar, the short lived Seventeenth Street Saloon on the site of what is now Blockbuster Video."

But being out and proud in Chelsea in the seventies was a dangerous proposition and a far cry from life twenty blocks south, in the Village. Shernoff describes the precautions gay men and lesbians took while outside in Chelsea: "We did not walk on the west side of Eighth Avenue between sunset and sunrise and avoided Ninth Avenue altogether if possible because of a gang of teenage bashers who roamed the neighborhood. Walking to The Eagle or [The] Spike, we either walked north up West Street or west along 23rd Street until Twelfth Avenue and then south again."

Down in the Village, even amid constant harassment from the police, gay culture—and gay bars—thrived. Popular spots like Ty's—still open and in its original location at 114 Christopher Street—Badlands, Peter Rabbit, Sneakers, and the International Stud opened during the West Village gay renaissance.

The common denominator for gay bars throughout the city in the 1970s were the backrooms. In many cases it seemed that the sale of liquor over the bar was a front for the real purpose of the neighborhood bars—tricking in the backroom. For many it was the safe alternative to the darkness and unpredictability of the piers and trucks.

But even the bars weren't always safe, as the gay community learned on the cold night of Wednesday, November 19, 1980. At ten o'clock that night, a man by the name of Ronald Crumpley got in his Cadillac and drove to the Ramrod on West Street. He walked up to two men standing near the bar and shot them point-blank with a .357 magnum. John Preston, writing for the December 1980 issue of *Alternate*, described what followed. "Then [Crumpley] walked back to the Cadillac and took out an Uzi machine gun....He crouched on the sidewalk and took careful aim at Little Dutch, the doorman who sat in the window, his usual spot. In a matter of seconds, more than 75 rounds crashed through the windows of the bar killing two men and wounding two more." One of the men killed was the doorman, whose real name was Jörg Wenz. The other man was never identified.

Testifying in his own defense at his trial, Crumpley claimed to believe that gay men were agents of the devil who were stalking him and were "trying to steal my soul* just by looking at me." He was found not guilty by reason of insanity and sent to Kirby Forensic Psychiatric Center.

The Baths

In *Gay New York, 1890–1940*, Chauncey explains that public bathhouses first appeared in New York City in 1852, encouraged and sponsored by an organization called the New York Association for the Improvement of the Condition of the Poor. The provision of public bathhouses was an attempt to "encourage cleanliness in the tenement districts," where "only one in forty families lived in a house or tenement with a bathroom."†

Though the first public bath was not a successful enterprise and closed shortly after it opened, by the 1890s, the association began opening baths with a new vigor. By 1915, sixteen public baths dotted the city in addition to a slew of Jewish baths and private Russian and Turkish baths—the first of such establishments to cater to Manhattan's middle class. Though it is known that gay sex among men did occur at the public baths, a tight watch was kept on patrons in order to discourage such behavior. In those days it was much more common for gay men who met at the public baths to make arrangements to meet elsewhere.

Chauncey points to two particular types of bathhouses where, by the 1920s, gay men enjoyed a little bit of freedom in expressing their sexual desires: "baths visited by straight as well as gay men but whose management tolerated limited homosexual activity, and those that catered to gay men by excluding nonhomosexual patrons and creating an environment in which homosexual activity was encouraged and safeguarded."* The former, in return for the increase in revenue from the gay clientele, allowed a little bit of action in the showers or steam rooms as long as it didn't raise the suspicions of other patrons or lead to the involvement of the police. The latter type of bathhouse was much harder to find. The three mentioned in Chauncey's history are the Ariston Baths, in the basement of the Ariston Apartment Hotel, on the northeast corner of Broadway and West Fifty-fifth Street. This was probably the city's first gay oriented bathhouse; it began operation around 1900. The other two, Stauch's and Claridge's, were on Coney Island and were popular in the 1930s.

Beginning in the 1950s, exclusively gay bathhouses began to crop up in America, a significant number of them located in New York City. Like gay bars, the baths were the targets of raids from the police department, though less frequently, as they were seen as "discreet outlets for the vast homosexual life in the city."

It wasn't until the late 1960s and throughout the 1970s that gay bathhouses became fully licensed establishments and began to thrive. Evolving from clandestine cruising grounds to beautiful and enormous structures offering everything from restaurants and gyms to massage parlors and dance floors, for many, the baths were truly the cornerstone of the gay social and sexual scene during that time. The famed activist and writer Larry Kramer told the author in an interview for the film *Gay Sex in the 70s*, "The easiest and most comfortable place† to be [during that time], quite frankly, was the baths. It was like going to a candy store."

Many of the baths in New York became legendary. The Everard Baths on West Twenty-eighth Street opened to the public on May 3, 1888; by the time it closed 97 years later, in 1985, it was New York's longest-running gay-oriented business. Gay men began frequenting the Everard Baths around the time of World War I, and it had established itself as a predominantly homosexual bathhouse by the 1920s. By the 1970s, it was one of the most popular gay bathhouses in the city and thrived despite a fire that ripped through the complex in 1977, killing nine men and injuring several more.

The St. Mark's Baths, which opened at 6 St. Mark's Place in 1915, made the transition from a bathhouse serving older Jewish men to a bathhouse serving exclusively homosexual men in the 1960s. (Some report that that transition began in the 1950s, when the St. Mark's began catering to gay men at night.) The St. Mark's, known to cater to a hard-core S&M crowd and thought to be one of the unclean and unsanitary bathhouses in the city, got a makeover in 1979. That year it was purchased by Bruce Mailman, owner of the legendary disco The Saint; he rehabbed it to eliminate the structure's liabilities and had the place redone with a "stylish" and "high-tech" feel. Of the renovation Mailman said, "Our approach was to make people comfortable enough that they would not need to sign in under a false name or run into someone there they knew." With the renovation, St. Mark's was touted as "the largest bathhouse in the country,"* boasting "three floors, a pool, roof deck, a steam room with shipboard portholes, 162 private rooms, and 250 lockers."

TIP The Everard Baths were said to be a favorite of the movie star Rock Hudson. According to the historical website gaytubs.com, even before AIDS had crept onto the scene, management of the New St. Mark's Baths handed out condoms, in a package that read "What's in this could save your life," and safe-sex pamphlets to the clients. Then, after the onset of AIDS, anyone entering the facility was required to sign a contract agreeing to practice safe sex.

The Continental Baths were opened by entrepreneur Steve Ostrow in the basement of the Upper West Side's landmark 1903 building the Ansonia Hotel in the late 1960s. In stark contrast to downtown's notoriously unclean bathhouses, the Continental Baths, with their extravagant accommodations, was advertised as being "reminiscent of the glory days of Rome." Featuring a disco dance floor, a cabaret lounge, sauna rooms, a swimming pool, and a clean, spacious facility, the bathhouse could accommodate nearly a thousand men and operated twenty-four hours a day.

TIP It was at the Continental Baths that Bette Midler met Barry Manilow, the man who would become her musical director and lifelong friend.

Though initially the draw to the Continental Baths was the sexual freedom it provided, for many, sex was trumped in 1970 when the then-unknown performer Bette Midler took the place by storm with her cabaret act. Midler, who was known to circulate a basket of poppers during her shows, was an instant hit among most of the men of the bathhouse. Her popularity and that of other performers, however, were detrimental to business, as they distracted the clientele from the serious business of sex. The writer Edmund White has said of Midler's effect at the Continental, "I was so sex-obsessed* that I found it irritating when she [Midler] was there because everybody stopped their sexual activities to listen to her. I was the person fuming away in the background, hoping everybody would hurry up and get back to work!"

By 1974, as Midler rose to national stardom and her shows at the baths were being attended by the likes of Shirley Maclaine, gay patronage fell off. Ostrow, in hopes of resurrecting his business, ended the cabaret acts and made the facility co-ed. But his efforts were to no avail and the Continental Baths closed for good in 1974 (but reopened in 1977 as Plato's Retreat).

TIP

The Continental Baths eventually reopened as a heterosexual swingers' club called Plato's Retreat. It was shut down by the City of New York at the height of the AIDS epidemic.

By 1985, health officials were becoming convinced that the unsafe sex practices taking place at the bathhouses were partially responsible for the rapid spread of AIDS, and they closed down most bathhouses in the city. Susan Tompkin, the assistant to Bruce Mailman at the New St. Mark's, remembered the day city health department personnel came to close the bathhouse in her interview with the author of *Gay Sex in the 70s*. "There was no door lock," she said. "They had to go out and get a padlock when the city said, 'Lock it up' because we never locked the door. There was no key. From the day the bath opened until the city closed it...it went 24 hours a day, 7 days a week."

Q-Review

Bruce Mailman. Owner of the legendary disco the Saint and the New St. Mark's Baths. For a number of years after the closing of the bathhouse he battled the city in court, arguing that the closure constituted an invasion of the patrons' right to privacy and freedom of association. The fight was never successful.

CHAPTER FIVE

The Response to AIDS

QUOTE

"Our continued existence as gay men upon the face of this earth is at stake. Unless we fight for our lives, we shall die. In all the history of homosexuality we have never been so close to death and extinction. Many of us are dying or are already dead."

—Larry Kramer, "1,112 and Counting"

BY THE mid-1970s, huge advances were being made toward establishing Chelsea as a safe neighborhood for the growing number of gays and lesbians who were moving there. Groups like the Chelsea Gay Association

(CGA),* the city's first gay and lesbian neighborhood group, began to work up an alliance with the police officers of the West Village's Sixth Precinct and Chelsea's Tenth Precinct. Officers in those neighborhoods who notoriously allowed for the harassment and violence against its gay residents were put through CGA's sensitivity training. All the while the new gay vigilante group SMASH (Society to Make America Safe for Homosexuals)—a group of about seven leather men tired of being beaten up and feeling fearful in their own neighborhood—patrolled the streets, first on foot and then, in order to cover more ground, in cars. They snared neighborhood gangs by sending decoys into dangerous areas. When they were jumped by the gangs, usually a handful of teenage thugs, members of SMASH would rush to the scene and beat the bashers. The decoys were so successful that within a week the chief of police called to tell the group that the gang leaders wanted a truce.

All was going well in the struggle for gay equality in New York City as the 1970s gave way to the 1980s. No longer a theoretical concept, the change—to full recognition of their civil rights—that gays and lesbians had been fighting for since Stonewall was palpable. And with a momentum that grew every day, it seemed that nothing could get in the movement's way. But then, the city's gay men mysteriously began to die as the silent plague we would come to call AIDS ravaged its way through their bodies.

Although the virus would become the most devastating and heartbreaking scourge the community had ever faced, later many reflected that it also became our greatest unifying force. And as always, a handful of voices emerged among the chaos to guide us along that journey.

Gay Men's Health Crisis (GMHC)

In his 1978 novel *Faggots*, Larry Kramer's protagonist, Fred Lemish, exclaims, "I've lived all over the world and I haven't seen more than half a dozen couples who have what I want….It tells me that no relationship in the world can survive the shit we lay on it….If those happy couples are there, they better come out of the woodwork fast and show themselves pronto so we can have a few examples for unbelieving heathens like you that it's possible. Before you fuck yourself to death."

Lemish, speaking to a cheating lover, was really Kramer expressing his frustrations with what he saw as a sex-obsessed gay community. But the warning, which came a full two years before anybody in the community became aware of the burgeoning virus, either fell on deaf ears or was lost amid the controversy unleashed by the book's publication. Kramer, who had been nominated for an Academy Award for his screenplay adaptation of the book *Women in Love*, ran in the social circles of New York's gay elite, but he found himself ostracized in the wake of *Faggots*. Even worse, as his friends began to die from the mysterious, heretofore extremely rare skin cancer called Kaposi's sarcoma, was the Cassandra complex that came along with his inference, long before it was proved by science, that the virus causing the cancer was a communicable disease being spread through the gay community by unprotected sex. Also apparent to

Q TIP When Larry Kramer's *Faggots* was first published, Oscar Wilde Memorial Bookshop owner Craig Rodwell refused to stock the book because he thought it was offensive to the gay community.

Kramer was the fact that the gay community was going to have to take care of its own.

On August 11, 1981, at the request of Dr. Alvin Friedman-Kien, a professor of dermatology and microbiology at New York University and the city's leading medical expert on the previously extremely rare cancer, Kramer called a meeting at his apartment on Fifth Avenue. According to Randy Shilts's depiction of the scene in his book *And the Band Played On: Politics, People, and the AIDS Epidemic*, "None of the political crazies were there. Present, instead, were la crème de la crème of New York's A-list gay nightlife, the hottest guys you'd see on the island or at the trendiest discos."[*] If anybody was going to be able to raise money and awareness, it was these men, many of whom had already lost friends to the illness or had become sick with it themselves.

Friedman-Kien spoke to the assembled men that night,[†] presenting his "tip-of-the-iceberg" theory: that the small number of people who had gotten sick and died up to that point were just the beginning. "He didn't know what was causing the epidemic," Shilts wrote, "but he knew that the people who got sick had lots of sex partners and had a long history of VD....The word needed to get out, Friedman-Kien warned; people needed to take it seriously. The doctor added that he needed money for research—now." That night, after Dr. Friedman-Kien left, a hat was passed around and $6,635 was collected from those present. Says Shilts, "That was just about all the private money to be raised to fight the new epidemic for the rest of the year."

The following week, Kramer, who had become almost instantly passionate about the new cause, wrote a personal appeal to the readers of the *New York Native*, New York's gay newspaper, which appeared in the August 24, 1981, issue and read in part:

> The majority of Kaposi['s] cases are being tended to at New York University Medical Center. The doctor who is most on top of this situation is there, Dr. Alvin Friedman-Kien.
>
> Money is desperately needed, both for their research, which is going on around the clock, and for the treatment and chemotherapy of many of the patients who have no money or medical insurance.
>
> I hope you will write a check and get your friends to write one too. This is our disease and we must take care of each other and ourselves. In the past we have often been a divided community; I hope we can all get together on this emergency, undivided, cohesively, and with all the numbers we in so many ways possess.

The *New York Native* was the only newspaper in New York City that gave thorough coverage to the AIDS in the early days of the epidemic. Many gay men and lesbians, unaware of how devastating the epidemic would become, dubbed the newspaper "the AIDS paper" and simply refused to read it.

On September 7, 1981,* Labor Day, two weeks following the publication of the Kramer's appeal in the *New York Native*, he and a handful of the men who had attended the meeting at his apartment hung a banner that read "Give To Gay Cancer" above a card table on the dock of the Pines side of Fire Island. The men who sat beneath the banner believed that this would be the best way to rally their gay brothers into donating to the cause. They were sure they would raise thousands of dollars. But their hopes were almost immediately dashed as person after person, en route to the party at the Ice Palace, the Pines' biggest and most famous dance club, either ignored or insulted the men, calling them hysterical or, as Shilts reported, accusing them of "participating in a heterosexual plot to undermine the gay community." The sum total of the weekend's efforts was $124.

Back in the city, the group, who had started called themselves and their initiative Gay Men's Health Crisis, made it official. The founding members were Larry Kramer, Nathan Fain, Dr. Lawrence Mass, Paul Popham, Paul Rapoport, and Edmund White. Popham, known for his good looks and for being at the pinnacle of New York's gay A-listers, was elected the group's first president. Kramer, a radical force by nature, was surprised and disappointed by the group's choice. Kramer disagreed with Popham's passive politics and his notion that "GMHC should not *tell* people anything, not in any way make up their minds for them." From that point forward, Kramer was at tactical odds with Popham and the board of directors; in his book *Reports from the Holocaust*, Kramer wrote that the board of directors "felt that softer tactics were required. 'You get more with honey than with vinegar' was the modus operandi that was urged upon me regularly.'"

But Kramer, furious that Mayor Ed Koch would not meet with the group and at the continued lethargy on the part of the Manhattan's gay community, insisted that militancy was the way to go. Kramer's boldest move in his quest to mobilize the community at the time was the writing of the article "1,112 and Counting," which appeared in the March 14, 1983, issue of the *New York Native*. The number 1,112 refers to the number of AIDS-related deaths that had occurred up to that point. It begins:

> If this article doesn't scare the shit out of you, we're in real trouble. If this article doesn't rouse you to anger, fury, rage, and action, gay men may have no

future on this earth. Our continued existence depends on just how angry you can get.

I am writing as Larry Kramer, and I am speaking for myself, and my views are not to be attributed to Gay Men's Health Crisis.

I repeat: Our continued existence as gay men upon the face of this earth is at stake. Unless we fight for our lives, we shall die. In all the history of homosexuality we have never been so close to death and extinction. Many of us are dying or are already dead.

Kramer goes on to outline the misconceptions of how the disease is transmitted, using actual graphic language common among gay men. He went on to debunk the myth that only a single "type" of gay man gets the disease and described how the inaction of both the government and gay people to push for research had left both groups with blood on their hands. The end of the article is a call to action:

It is necessary that we have a pool of at least 3,000 people who are prepared to participate in demonstrations of civil disobedience. Such demonstrations might include sit-ins or traffic tie-ups. All participants must be prepared to be arrested. I am asking every gay person and every gay organization to canvass all friends and members and make a count of the total number of people you can provide towards this pool of 3,000.

The article was reproduced in just about every gay newspaper and magazine in the country. It has gone down in history as one of the most important documents in the history of the AIDS epidemic.

"1,112 and Counting" was exactly the kind of in-your-face candor that Popham and the board of GMHC were afraid of. According to Kramer, GMHC hated the article and insisted on inserting into the second paragraph a disclaimer to the effect that they had nothing to do with it. The article's publication was the beginning of the end of Kramer's association with the group. The final rupture came when GMHC was finally granted their meeting with Mayor Koch and the board told Kramer that he was not invited to attend. They were afraid he would embarrass the organization by yelling at the mayor. Kramer threatened to resign if they didn't change their position. When the board didn't budge, Kramer followed through and left the group.

Response to Kramer's call to action didn't produce much and was a disappointment. As he tells it, "A group of about fifty managed to coalesce and meet for instruction [on outreach] with a straight black man who had worked with Martin Luther King Jr. We called ourselves the AIDS Network Public Events Committee. Such a small number didn't augur well. But," he writes with knowing foresight, "as will be seen it proved to be sufficient."*

GMHC is still a vibrant organization that offers an array of services to thousands of men, women, and children every year regardless of HIV status or sexual orientation. They respond to over 35,000 phone calls and Internet requests yearly in both Spanish and English with accurate information, emotional support, and an expansive referral service that includes over 10,000 service providers.

TIP In the early 1980s the illness that was killing gays was called GRID (Gay Related Immune Deficiency), then ACIDS (Acquired Community Immune Deficiency Syndrome) and CAIDS (Community Acquired Immune Deficiency Syndrome). The epidemic finally got its official name, AIDS (Acquired Immune Deficiency Syndrome), on July 27, 1982.

Years later, Kramer would remember with fondness the group's early days for his book *Reports from the Holocaust*:

> Paul Popham and I...supervised the daily running of the organization. For both of us it became a consuming passion—helping, urging, nurturing, watching this small group develop, at first falteringly, but then beginning to grow as increasing numbers of dedicated men and women came to join us. It was one of those rare moments in life when one felt completely utilized, useful, with a true reason to be alive.*

The Normal Heart

And the Band Played On, Shilts's history of the impact of AIDS on the gay community, follows Kramer on a trip he took to Europe in July 1983—a little over two years after the first meeting in his apartment—also the first fundraiser—of the group that would come to be known as Gay Men's Health Crisis. In Munich, with nothing but time on his hands, Kramer saw a sign that said "Dachau." Intrigued, he headed for the town, and a few hours later found himself standing in front of one of World War II's most infamous concentration camps. He found out while touring the museum that the camp was opened in 1933, almost immediately after Hitler took power. It didn't make sense to him that the camp could have been operating a full eight years before the United States entered the war. How could we have let that happen? But then all too quickly, the picture became clear. It mirrored exactly what was happening then in the United States with the AIDS epidemic—the general population didn't care because so far it hadn't affected them directly. The realization made Kramer furious; all at once, as Shilts tells it, he knew what he had to do. Write a play about what was happening in New York.

Kramer has said of his decision to write a play that writing a book would have taken too long, with the lengthy editing process that all books require, and that writing a film was out of the question because getting a film on the subject made would have been virtually impossible. A play could be written fast and, though it was sure to reach a smaller audience at first than a book or film, it had the added emotional impact of being live and in-your-face. So he left Europe and set off for Cape Cod, where he was quickly able to rent a cottage on the beach and get to work.*

His intention was to make people cry. The best way to do that, he decided, was to tell the truth about the AIDS epidemic. So he modeled the main character, Ned Weeks, on himself and set about telling his own story. We watch Ned take part in the founding of "The Organization"—an AIDS activism group modeled on GMHC—only to split with the group when he isn't invited to the much-awaited meeting with the mayor. And we watch as Ned finally finds true love in the form of Felix Turner, a reporter for the *New York Times*, only to watch him get sick with the disease and ultimately die from it. In the play, Bruce Niles, president of The Organization, is modeled on Paul Popham, and Dr. Emma Brookner, who is desperate in her attempt to help the AIDS victims while at the same time trying to get them to change the behaviors that put them at risk, is based on his real-life friend Dr. Linda Laubenstein.

He had settled on the title *City of Death*, before deciding that was too dark and changing it to *The Normal Heart*; he borrowed the phrase from a W. H. Auden poem, "September 1, 1939."

The Normal Heart opened on April 21, 1985, at the Public Theater, with Brad Davis in the starring role as Ned. It was an instant hit. Almost immediately, productions of the play were mounted in Los Angeles, starring Richard Dreyfuss; in New Haven, with Tom Hulce; and

TIP *The Normal Heart* was revived
by the Public Theater in 2004 in
the same space where it was
originally produced. The show
starred Tony winner Joanna
Gleason as Dr. Emma Brookner
and Raul Esparza as Ned Weeks.

in London, with Martin Sheen. Though it was not the
first play with an AIDS theme to be produced in this
country—that distinction is held by William M. Hoffman's *As Is*, which had opened a little less than two
months earlier—more than twenty years after its original run it still holds the record for being the longest-
running show at the Public Theater. And because the
play functions essentially as a time capsule in its telling
of the early years of the AIDS epidemic in New York
city—almost like a documentary—it has earned the distinction of being one of the most important historical
plays of the twentieth century.

At the end of the play, as the stage lights slowly fade
to black over Felix's deathbed, Ned is being comforted
by his brother. In the darkness, Ned lets out a howl
filled with pain and frustration—a howl that is the true
embodiment of Kramer's rage against the disease.
"AIDS," he has said, "is the saddest thing I'll ever have
to know."*

ACT UP

On the morning of March 24, 1987, more than 250 men and women descended on Wall Street in lower Manhattan.* The goal was simple, to protest the actions of the Federal Drug Administration and its chief, Dr. Frank Young, for their unconscionable failure to speed the approval and distribution of promising drugs to aid the more than 32,000 people living with HIV/AIDS in the United States. The protesters tied up traffic and distributed more than ten thousand fact sheets about the FDA "horror show" as well as an op-ed piece from the *New York Times* by Larry Kramer on the crimes committed against HIV/AIDS patients by the FDA. The protesters also hanged Dr. Young in effigy outside Trinity Church. The action was met with wild applause.

A few weeks later Dr. Young made some promises on the evening news about speeding the testing and releasing processes for new drugs. Dan Rather gave the credit

Dr. Larry Mass, the First Writer to Report on the Epidemic Later Known as AIDS

MAY 18, 1981, was the day the world first heard the news about a disease that would become the epidemic we call AIDS. It was in an article by Dr. Larry Mass called "Disease Rumors Largely Unfounded," published that week in New York's gay newspaper, the *New York Native*.

"Following that first report in May," Mass later wrote, "it was almost immediately clear that we were dealing with a public health emergency." He quickly gathered the pieces of information he had into his first feature article on the disease, "Cancer in the Gay Community," which he published the following month. The piece, which ran almost two entire pages, was published at a time when both mainstream and gay media were all but ignoring the issue. In fact, the article has been deemed so historically relevant that it has become part of the permanent displays of the Newseum, the Museum of Journalism and Media, in Arlington, Virginia.

While continuing to write an almost weekly column for the *Native* over the next year, publishing more than twenty-three articles, Mass was also a driving force behind the grassroots efforts to make the government take notice of the disease. Larry Kramer, founder of both Gay Men's Health Crisis and ACT UP, once wrote, "When the first article appeared in the *New York Times*, saying that Dr. Alvin Friedman-Kien and Dr. Linda Laubenstein at New York University were reporting 41 cases of severe disease among gay men, Larry Mass encouraged me to investigate." Mass, a close friend of Kramer's, was there the night Friedman-Kien spoke to the group in Kramer's apartment and was one of the cofounders of GMHC.

Recently, as historians look back at the early reporting on AIDS, Mass has taken some flack for the less-than-urgent approach he seemed to be taking in his reporting in the early days. Mass defends his tactics, however. On the twenty-fifth anniversary of the naming of the disease, in a feature article in *Newsweek*, the writer David Jefferson credits Mass with writing the first article on AIDS, only to point out that "even the gay press got it wrong." Mass has written, "It would be easy for me to concede Jefferson's point but minimize my own culpability by blaming *Native* editor and publisher Charles Ortleb for choosing the headline [for the first article]. But I'm not sure that that's what happened....The one goal that sustained me throughout my early reporting on AIDS was to tell the truth, no matter how impolitic, how untimely, how unpopular."

Dr. Mass is still a major figure in AIDS education and awareness.

to the new activist group, which had its coming-out party that day on Wall Street. They were called ACT UP, or the AIDS Coalition to Unleash Power.

It all started a few weeks prior on the evening of March 10, 1987, when the writer and producer Nora Ephron—scheduled to speak that night at the Gay and Lesbian Center's monthly speaker's series—got the flu. Scrambling to find a replacement, the director of the program called Larry Kramer and asked him to fill in. "I had no idea what I wanted to talk about," Kramer wrote later. "I thought I'd said everything I had to say or could say—too many times. There didn't seem to be anything new to talk about."* But after a visit to Houston, Texas, to see a production of his play *The Normal Heart* and visit the Institute for Immunological Disorders, he realized how wrong he had been. He knew he had to tell whoever came to hear him speak that it was time to fight back.

Roughly 250 people packed the center's main lecture hall that night. A hush came over the crowd as Kramer approached the podium, took a deep breath, and began.

On March 14, 1983, almost four years ago to this
date, I wrote an article for the *New York Native*.
There were at that time 1,112 cases of AIDS nation-
wide....There are now officially—and we all know
how officials count—32,000 with 10,000 of these in
New York....

I sometimes think we have a death wish. I think
we must want to die. I have never been able to understand why for six long years we have sat back
and literally let ourselves be knocked off man by
man—without fighting back. I have heard of denial,
but this is more than denial; it *is* a death wish.*

Kramer went on to tell the audience about his experi-
ence in Texas—visiting the country's very first AIDS hospital, the Institute for Immunological Disorders. Kramer
described it as the "the most wonderful AIDS hospital in
the world," run by Dr. Peter Marshall, "one of the top
AIDS doctors in America." The Institute, able to treat 150
patients, had only 16. Kramer explained that that was because "Texas is the only state in the country where if you
don't have insurance, where if you're indigent, the state
will not reimburse you or the hospital for the cost of your
care." Most of the infected in Texas didn't have insurance,
which meant that they couldn't go to the hospital and the
wonderful facility was going largely unused.

Kramer went after the FDA next. He told horror stories
about double-blind studies for potentially life-saving
drugs in which half the group—most of whom were desperate to take anything with promise—was given the drug
while the other half got a placebo. Neither group knew
who got what until the study was over, a period of time

that was often six months to a year or longer. He spoke of the bureaucracy involved with getting drugs even to be considered for testing by the FDA and the selfishness of the major companies, which planned to market the drugs for tens of thousands of dollars per year per patient.

Near the end of his speech, Kramer said, "Every one of us here is capable of doing something. Of doing something strong. We have to go after the FDA—fast. That means coordinated protests, pickets, arrests." This idea struck a cord with the crowd, who, after "much discussion," decided to hold another meeting three days later. It is estimated that 300 or more people showed up at that meeting—the meeting that would ultimately see the founding of ACT UP. In *Reports from the Holocaust* Kramer described the group's initial function as being "an ad-hoc community protest group that was pledged to concentrate on fighting for the release of experimental drugs."

As with Gay Men's Health Crisis, Kramer found himself at odds with the direction ACT UP was going in soon after its inception. But rather than stay and fight it out, he decided to leave the group quietly while still showing up at demonstrations when he could.

ACT UP remained a vital organization throughout the late 1980s and into the 1990s, drawing young gay and lesbian people from all around the country to New York City to join the group. At its peak, the organization had thousands of members in more than seventy chapters across the globe.

Though ACT UP is no longer the vital institution it once was, many chapters still exist, including the original one here in New York City.

ACT UP's Achievements

- 1988. ACT UP's Women's Caucus organizes first ACT UP action focused on women and HIV. Five hundred people protest an article telling heterosexual women that unprotected vaginal intercourse with an HIV-positive man is safe. A documentary about the action, called *Doctors, Liars, and Women: AIDS Activists Say NO to Cosmo*, tours the country before being placed in the permanent collection of the Museum of Modern Art.

- 1989. ACT UP makes history by stopping trading on the Stock Exchange floor. Seven members infiltrate the NYSE and chain themselves to the VIP balcony. Their miniature foghorns drown out the opening bell, and a banner unfurls above the trading floor demanding "SELL WELCOME." Other members snap photos which they then sneak out and send over the news-wires. Four days later,

Burroughs Wellcome lowers the price of [the drug] AZT by 20 percent, to $6,400 per year.

- 1991. ACT UP targets President Bush at the White House, declaring that, with over 120,000 Americans dead from AIDS, the president is getting away with murder. In a loud and angry march to the White House, activists demanded that the president stop his deliberate policy of neglect. Eighty-four people were arrested in acts of civil disobedience that included chaining themselves to the gates of the White House and to each other. Bush spent the day at Disney World.

- 1992: ACT UP member Rob Rafsky confronts candidate Bill Clinton at a New York City fundraiser. Clinton asks what he should be saying to prove that he cares about AIDS. The exchange is carried on CNN and ABC's *Nightline*.

- 1993. In the third political funeral for a member of ACT UP NY, the coffin of Jon Greenburg, thirty-seven, was carried through the streets of the East Village to Tompkins Square Park, where personal eulogies were heard by more than 200 activists, friends, and family members. "I don't want an angry political funeral," wrote Greenberg. "I just want you to burn me in the street and eat my flesh."

- 1994. ACT UP launches *ACT UP LIVE!*, a weekly call-in show on Manhattan public-access TV.[*]

Q-Review

Larry Kramer. The world's most famous AIDS activist. Kramer was nominated for an Academy Award in 1969 for his screenplay of *Women in Love*. He is the author of the bestseller *Faggots* as well as the play *The Normal Heart* and its sequel *The Destiny of Me*, among others. He is a cofounder of Gay Men's Health Crisis and ACT UP.

Dr. Lawrence Mass. An AIDS activist and writer, Mass is best known for his coverage of the AIDS epidemic for the *New York Native*. He is credited with writing the world's first article on what would come to be called AIDS, for the May 18, 1981, edition of the *New York Native*. He is one of the cofounders of Gay Men's Health Crisis.

Paul Popham. A cofounder and the first president of Gay Men's Health Crisis. Popham died in 1987 of AIDS-related complications.

Edmund White. Cofounder of Gay Men's Health Crisis. White is also the noted author of *The Joy of Gay Sex: An Intimate Guide for Gay Men to the Pleasures of a Gay Life; States of Desire: Travels in Gay America; A Boy's Own Story;* and *My Lives*.

Dr. Linda Laubenstein. A close friend of Larry Kramer's, Dr. Laubenstein was the inspiration for the character Dr. Emma Brookner in his play *The Normal Heart*. Laubenstein was a renowned AIDS researcher who discovered some of the first cases of AIDS. A paraplegic since the age of five, she died in 1992 at the age of forty-five from complications stemming from childhood polio.

CHAPTER SIX

Pride

"Until the day all gay, lesbian, bisexual, and transgendered people can live their lives without violence, harassment, and discrimination, they must continue to *march* openly and proudly."

—Phil Mannino, of Heritage of Pride

AS THE 1980s gave way to the 1990s, it seemed as though real progress in the quest for GLBT equality was being made. The number of Pride celebrations seemed to be increasing markedly around the country as, each year in June, smaller cities and towns joined in the chorus of the bigger metropolises championing equal rights. It seemed only right that New York City, the birthplace of the celebration, would lead the charge in making its annual Pride traditions official by creating an

The Q Guide to NYC Pride

organization dedicated solely to preserving and carrying on the legacy started by Craig Rodwell and the Christopher Street Liberation Day Committee. Thus, Heritage of Pride was born.

Heritage of Pride (HOP)

The U.S. Federal Archives Building on the corner of Christopher and Greenwich streets towers above any other building in that section of the West Village. The building, now consisting primarily of apartments, is rumored to be the home of celebrities such as Monica Lewinsky and Christina Ricci; it also houses a chain gym and an off-Broadway theater. Down in the basement is a one-room office full of file cabinets and fluorescent lighting, and this is where Heritage of Pride volunteers plan the events for New York City's Pride Week—one of the largest Pride celebrations in the world. Considering that almost 800,000 visitors attend the annual rally in Bryant Park, the march down Fifth Avenue, and the dance on Pier 20, it seems remarkable that so much planning could be done in one little room.

Heritage of Pride calls itself "a wholly volunteer-managed, non-partisan, tax-exempt, not-for-profit corporation that organizes Lesbian, Gay, Bisexual and Transgender Pride events in New York City to commemorate and celebrate the Stonewall Riots." The organization was founded in 1984 by Mark Berkeley, Matt Foreman, Candida Scott Piel, and Brian O'Dell. The four had been members of the Christopher Street Liberation Day Committee, the organization that had been planning the rally and the march since 1970, when Craig

Rodwell put the group together. The group was tired of the year-to-year character of CSLDC, with no formal ongoing structure. In light of how Pride events in New York were attracting more and more people each year, the group officially dissolved what was left of the CSLDC and started Heritage of Pride. The hope was that a formal organization could more effectively maximize the potential of Pride. They got to work immediately, focusing their attention on the four Pride events that still take place today.

First is the rally. Held since 1997 in Bryant Park, behind the New York Public Library at Fifth Avenue and Forty-second Street, the rally commemorates the event that took place one month to the day after the Stonewall Riot. On June 30, 1970, about 500 people gathered in Washington Square Park for a "Gay Power" demonstration. That event, the very first New York City Pride Rally, was followed by a candlelight vigil in Sheridan Square. In the three decades since, the rally has known several different homes, including Union Square Park and various parts of Central Park. In recent years this event has drawn upwards of 10,000 attendees.

The second event is the march, which draws over 600,000 people to the streets annually. The route is from Fifty-third Street downtown, and ends up at the corner of Christopher and Greenwich streets. Though it is one of the most festive queer events of the year, HOP views it as a protest. In the spirit of the events put on by their predecessor, the Christopher Street Liberation Day Committee, "HOP feels that until the day all gay, lesbian, bisexual, and transgendered people can live their lives without violence, harassment, and discrimination,

they much continue to *march* openly and proudly."* In
the middle of the march, there is a pause for two minutes of silence in commemoration of all those who have
died of AIDS.

The third is the Pier Dance—an event on Pier 20 that
draws over 7,000 people each year. The idea of the dance
was born of a time when our community could not
dance openly and proudly with other members of the
community. Organizers call it a protest set to music, "a
celebration set to the western skyline and a reminder of
how far we've come these last two decades."†

The fourth major annual Pride event is PrideFest, a
street festival held at the end of the march on the section
of Greenwich Avenue and Washington Street between
Christopher and Spring Streets. PrideFest comprises
four events: MarketPlace, a market where attendees are
encouraged to get a bite to eat; ArtSpace, an open-air
gallery exhibiting one-of-a-kind and limited-edition
fine art, photography, and crafts by women and men in
the local and international LGBT community; Kid-
Space, a playground; and StageFest, a stage for live-mu-
sic performances.

In 1985, when New York City issued the first official
permit for the Pride March, Matt Forman, a Heritage of
Pride cofounder, petitioned the city to paint a lavender
line along the parade route. It was an idea taken from
the courtesy provided by the city to the planners of the
annual St. Patrick's day parade, for whom a green line is
painted along the route of the parade. The city complied
with Foreman's request and agreed to paint the lavender
line from the beginning of the parade route, at Fifty-sec-
ond and Fifth, down Fifth Avenue to Eighth Street, west

on Eighth to Greenwich Avenue, down Greenwich Avenue to Christopher Street, past the Stonewall Inn, to the conclusion of the march at the corner of Christopher and Greenwich streets. Then in 2005, the line was extended past the March route to include PrideFest. The lavender line is longer than the St. Patrick's Day parade line by almost a half mile and is more durable—sections of it can be seen well into the fall and early winter. People are encouraged by HOP to "adopt a block" along the parade route and make a small donation toward helping the organization put on the Pride events. Blocks can be dedicated to anyone and a complete list of all dedications is listed in the annual Pride Guide. The lavender line has become an annual tradition and is a vital symbol of New York City's Pride events since its inception.

In 1990, Heritage of Pride had its hand in another lavender milestone. After six long years of lobbying by HOP, the Gay and Lesbian Alliance against Defamation (GLAAD), and a handful of other gay rights groups, the Empire State Building's famous illuminated tower went lavender in honor of the anniversary of the Stonewall Riots and in celebration of Gay Pride weekend. The inclusion of the lavender light display in the skyscraper's program of lighting statements—for example, red, white, and blue for the Fourth of July; no light at all for the day without art/night without light AIDS awareness day—is a big honor, as the building's management receives hundreds of requests each year. A spokesman for the building's management company, Helmsley-Spear, stated that the company was in "total agreement" with "leaders who seek to end the bigotry and discrimination directed against gay and lesbian New Yorkers."

- Thanks to the efforts of Heritage of Pride, dozens of churches throughout the city ring their steeple bells during the annual Pride March's moment of silence to honor those who have been lost to AIDS.

- The first rainbow Pride flag was made by hand by San Francisco resident Gilbert Baker. He had copies of the flag made, and these were first flown at San Francisco Pride events in 1978. Heritage introduced the Pride flag to the East Coast in 1986.

- The origin of the inverted pink triangle, another modern-day symbol of GLBT pride, is the cloth patch that homosexual men in the concentration camps of Hitler's Third Reich were forced to wear. Lesbians, female dissidents, and prostitutes were forced to wear black triangles.

- Thanks to the efforts of Heritage of Pride, the section of Christopher Street between Sixth and Seventh Avenues—the site of the Stonewall Riots—has been declared a historical landmark. That block is now called Stonewall Place.

The Dyke March

On the evening of April 24, 1993, in Washington, DC, 20,000 lesbians marched up Pennsylvania Avenue to the White House.* They chanted slogans such as "Ten percent is not enough! Recruit! Recruit! Recruit!"—poking fun at the notion that homosexuals recruit young people to join their lifestyle and become gay. Some ate fire, a symbolic gesture meant to represent the taking back of power from those who attempted to destroy them. Some wore superhero capes, and others simply walked with the group, happy to be a part of the biggest lesbian demonstration in history.

It was the night before the National Gay and Lesbian Task Force's first march on Washington, which had drawn hundreds of thousands of lesbians and gay men from all over the country to march through the nation's capital to the White House in a show of force. But a small group of lesbians from New York City had devised a plan for an additional protest of their own. The Lesbian Avengers were a direct-action group, founded in the East Village in 1992, that came to be known for their in-your-face street-theater style of activism. They had heard of the march on Washington and knew the numbers of marchers it would attract, so they went to DC and spread the word that the night before, lesbians would have their own march. There would be no permit, no speakers, no permission from the police— rather, just a group of dykes marching in protest and showing their own strength in numbers.

The group was no stranger to controversy in their quest to "fight for lesbian visibility and survival." In their first action,* they demonstrated by marching in front of an elementary school in Queens in a notoriously conservative neighborhood wearing T-shirts bearing the message "I Was a Lesbian Child" while distributing lavender balloons with the words "Ask About Lesbian Lives." In the wake of the success of the march in Washington, the group went home and planned a march for the night before the Pride March in New York that June. Again, to maintain the spirit of the march as a protest and not a celebration, they did not apply for a permit. Rather, with a budget of just a few hundred dollars, they trained marshals, got the word out, and somehow organized the women who showed up along the Forty-second Street sidewalk. They marched on the sidewalk down Fifth Avenue—some were actually pushed on a bed, the march's one makeshift float—and of course they spilled into the street, where they kept on going until they reached Washington Square Park. It was disorganized and chaotic compared to the Heritage of Pride march, scheduled for the following day—and that was the point. They reveled in the fact that they could make such a statement with a fraction of the funding and manpower of HOP. They knew it was a groundbreaking event in the history of lesbian activism. In 2003, Sara Pursley, one of the original Lesbian Avengers and a planner of the march, wrote in an article in *Gay City News*, "It wasn't long ago, but it was before lesbians were on the cover of *Newsweek* and *Vanity Fair*, before lesbian chic, before niche marketing and Absolute Pride, before Ellen."

Lesbian Avengers was made up of a group of fire-crackers, and the organization, sadly, burned out almost as quickly as it got started. The group's small membership made the planning of demonstrations nearly impossible, and it began to decline by the end of 1994. But Pursley stayed true to the group to the end. "In 1995," she wrote gamely, "I attended what I believe to be the last Lesbian Avenger meeting—by myself. I smoked a cigarette and voted unanimously to disband the group."

But the Dyke March lives on. Now run by the Independent Dyke March Committee, it attracts a more diverse group of marchers—and more and more marchers in general—each year. Each year the committee refuses to apply for a permit, and each year the police try to tell the group that they will be restricted to the sidewalk. And each year, as the crowd pours off the sidewalk and into the street, they are given a little more than half of Fifth Avenue between Forty-second Street and Twenty-third Street and then all of Fifth Avenue between Twenty-third Street and Washington Square Park. One year, to save face on the issue, the police department issued a statement that the committee had applied for and been granted a permit for their parade route. Knowing it wasn't true, the committee asked to see a copy of the permit so as to find out who had applied. The permit, of course, was never delivered.

Except for the occasional scuffle between an aggressive police officer and a marcher trying to get into the street (such incidents are handled by the trained marshals), the marches have always gone off without a hitch. In fact, in the history of the march there have only been three known arrests.

Incarnations of New York's Dyke March have popped up in cities around the country.

What's Hot Now?

Is the Village over? Is Chelsea tired? Is the West Side's Hell's Kitchen—Helsea, as some are now calling it—the new place to be?

Though the answers to these questions remain to be seen, one thing is for certain—the era of the gay ghetto has passed as gay bars have started opening in just about every neighborhood in the city. Here are a few highlights.

The East Village

The Phoenix. Where the Williamsburg hipsters meet the East Village locals. Intimidating? Absolutely. But fun anyway. Known for its cheap drink specials, it's a favorite of queer celebrities like Kevin Aviance and Michael Cunningham. 447 East Thirteenth Street.

Starlight. Touted as "the best gay bar to bring your straight friends to." Sunday night is ladies' night and is considered to be one of the best lesbian parties in the city. 167 Avenue A.

B Bar. At B Bar, Beige, the Tuesday night A-list gay party, is still, believe it or not, rocking after all these years. Look for celebrities such as Boy George, George Michael, Amanda LePore, and David LaChapelle. 40 East Fourth Street.

The West Village

The Duplex. Everyone has to have a favorite piano bar...no? Well give this one a try. And check out the special events in their Cabaret Space (such as Kate Pazikis's Mostly Sondheim Fridays; if you can get her to sing it will be well worth the two-drink minimum). 61 Christopher Street.

Stonewall. Worth checking out for the history. If you have questions about the riot, talk to the bartender, Tree—he was there! And try not to be offended by the establishment's tag line—"Come to Stonewall where every night's a riot!" Don't look for celebrities here. 53 Christopher Street.

The Factory. The only independent coffee shop left on Christopher Street. It's a little dark, but has comfy chairs and plenty of space. It's rumored to be the coffee shop *Friends'* Central Perk is based on. 104 Christopher Street.

Kettle of Fish. Not a gay bar, but if you're out with your straight friends stop in for a pitcher of beer and a round of darts. The place has an incredibly welcoming atmosphere and the most comfortable couches in the city. 59 Christopher Street.

Julius'. Check out the oldest gay bar in the city. 159 West Tenth Street.

Henrietta Hudson. Celebrating fifteen years of being New York City's premiere lesbian bar. 483 Hudson at Morton Street.

Ruby Fruit Bar & Grill. 531 Hudson Street.

Chelsea

Gym Bar. The city's only gay sports bar and as far away from the typical Chelsea stand-and-pose scene as one can get. The friendliest bartenders around (Hey, Jorge!). And brightly lit enough so you can actually see how seriously these guys take their sport. 167 Eighth Avenue.

Splash. One of the only gay dance clubs left in the city, and voted best gay bar by most publications, like, a zillion times. You haven't lived until you've been to Splash's musical Mondays. 50 West Seventeenth Street.

Barracuda. Known for its unpretentiousness and for its great mix of guys. The week-night drag shows hosted by Candice Cain and Shequida draw a crowd, as do the weekend DJs. 275 West Twenty-second Street.

The Eagle. Technically north of Chelsea, this notoriously dark and, well, dirty leather landmark has been around since just after the Stonewall Riot. Let The Eagle speak for itself: "New York's premiere leather bar continues its tradition of having the hottest men, great pool tables, and serious cruising." 554 West Twenty-eighth Street.

Hell's Kitchen

Posh. Perhaps your best bet to meet and actually talk to new people in all of Hell's Kitchen. Charming with its exposed brick and cozy with its couch lounge in the back. Usually crowded and great for both after work or bar hopping in the middle of the night. 405 West Fifty-first Street.

Barrage. Best in the spring and summer when the entire front of the bar opens onto the street. Also, one of the only bars close to the theater district that does a post-theater happy hour from eleven to midnight. 401 West Forty-seventh Street.

Vlada. The bar that raises the bar for the Hell's Kitchen gay establishments. With its infusion martinis and the long strip of ice built into the main bar so patrons can keep their drinks cold, Vlada is packing them in nightly. Definitely worth stopping by on your pub crawl. 331 West Fifty-first Street.

The Upper West Side

Candle Bar. Pickings are slim in what used to be one of the hottest neighborhoods for gay bars. But Candle Bar is a good standby. Meet the local gays and check out the AMDA boys, if that's your thing. 309 Amsterdam Avenue.

Suite. On the corner of 109th Street and Amsterdam Avenue, almost fifty blocks from Midtown, Suite is breaking new ground by venturing so far uptown. Usually packed with Columbia University boys and their friends, its comfortable, lively, and moderately priced. 992 Amsterdam Avenue at 109th Street.

The Upper East Side

OW. Though the West Side is the traditional home of New York City's gay culture, OW (Oscar Wilde) is definitely worth the trip to the other side of Central Park. OW is like a slice of Chelsea—without the pretense—on the Upper East Side. Touted as "more fun than a bathtub full of Jell-O," OW has a smoking patio as well as the longest bar in the city. 221 East Fifty-eighth Street.

The Townhouse. For the older crowd. Known to be the city's only "gay gentlemen's club," the ownership says it was "designed to appreciate older men of exquisite taste along with those who admire them." 236 East Fifty-eighth Street.

Q-Review

Matt Foreman. One of the original founders of Heritage of Pride. He was the executive director of the Empire State Pride Agenda from 1997 to 2000. He was named the executive director of the National Gay and Lesbian Task Force in 2003.

Lesbian Avengers. An important, if short-lived, lesbian activist group. Active from 1992 to 1995, the group invented the Dyke March.

Sarah Pursley. An early member of Lesbian Avengers, Pursley helped coordinate the first Dyke Marches in both Washington, DC, and New York City. She wrote the article "A Brief History of the Dyke March According to Me" for the newspaper *Gay City News* in 2003.

Acknowledgments

I gratefully acknowledge that the writing of this book would not have been possible without the help, guidance, and support of the following people:

The early LGBT activists who did the work fearlessly and left behind a story worth telling.

The historians Martin Duberman and David Carter, whose work provided both insight and inspiration. Also, Randy Shilts, whose book *And The Band Played On* turned me on to LGBT history in the first place.

There is a special place in my heart for the librarians of the Archives and Manuscripts division of the New York Public Library. Their diligence and dedication makes books like these possible.

All those who provided invaluable insight by allowing me to interview them for this book, especially Tree, Storme DeLarverie, Kim Bristner, and Phil Mannino.

The incredible crew at Alyson Books, especially Shannon Berning, my editor, whose patience and belief in this project have meant the world to me.

My friends who've kept me going, especially Mike Jensen, Hawmi Guillebeaux, Lucas Hall, Ellyn Marsh, Kathleen McGhee, Maxie Max, Donna Moss, Mike Harpish, and Amaya Brecher. The CGNY team: You all keep this Mary giggling. And an extra special thanks to Lisa Hagan, my agent, who never ceases to believe in me.

Finally, to my family—my mom, Pam Parker, and her wife, Carol Jenney—for your patience, love, and support. My sister Sarah, her husband, Glenn, and their beautiful son, Griffin. My brother, Nick, and his gorgeous daughter, Tessa. And my sister Becca, who has made us all proud. I love you all.

Notes

Chapter 1. Downtown's Secret Gay Underworld

Page

3   On certain nights in the late 1950s: Tree, a Stonewall-era veteran, interviewed by author, May 5, 2006, at the Stonewall Inn. Interview transcript in possession of the author.

6   For nearly thirty years: Ibid.

6   In the heart of the West Village: David Carter, *Stonewall: The Riots That Sparked the Gay Revolution* (New York: St. Martin's Griffin, 2004), p. 11; see also Tree interview.

7   What they found when they got there: Carter, *Stonewall*, pp. 15–19.

7   "lewd and dissolute": Ibid., p. 48.

8   I've been tending and managing bars: Tree interview.

10   On the unseasonably warm afternoon: For an account of the process of repealing laws against serving drinks to gays, see Martin Duberman, *Stonewall* (New York: Dutton, 1994), pp. 114–17; Carter, *Stonewall*, pp. 49–51.

11   "disorderly and subject to closure": Carter, *Stonewall*, p. 17.

12   "Taking the button off…": This account of the meeting, and the wording of the sign, is from

Craig Rodwell, a Stonewall-era veteran, interview by Martin Duberman, 1990, transcript, series 4, box 12, Craig Rodwell Papers, New York Public Library (henceforth cited as Rodwell Papers). This is the wording that Rodwell recalls.

12 "We don't serve faggots": Rodwell interview.

12 "I, however, want to order a…": Ibid.

12 "file a complaint…": Carter, *Stonewall*, p. 49.

12 "Still sort of terrified…": Rodwell interview.

13 "I think it's the law": Carter, *Stonewall*, p. 50.

12 "This might be a matter…": Ibid., pp. 50–51.

14 "come within the bounds…": Ibid.

14 In the summer of 1966: On the history of the Oscar Wilde Memorial Bookshop, see Rodwell interview.

15 It was not only: "The Advocate and Oscar Wilde Memorial Bookstore," glbtq.com/literature/journalism_publishing,3 .html. glbtq.com is an online encyclopedia of gay, lesbian, bisexual, transgender, and queer culture.

19 On a breezy October night: Molly McGarry and Fred Wasserman, *Becoming Visible* (New York: Penguin Studio, 1998), pp. 144–46.

19 "The country, it seemed to me…": Jonathan Katz, *Gay American History: Lesbians and Gay Men in the USA* (New York: Plume), p. 614.

19 "a service and welfare organization…": Ibid., p. 142.

20 Kim Brinster: Kim Brinster, interview by author.

23 "In absence of valid evidence…": John D'Emilio, *Sexual Politics, Sexual Communities: The Making of a Homosexual Minority in the United States, 1940–1970* (Chicago: University of Chicago, 1998).

24 Years later Del Martin recalled: Del Martin and
    Phyllis Lyon, *Lesbian/Women* (rev. ed., New York:
    Bantam, 1983), pp. 238–39.
24 They might still be isolated geographically: Katz,
    Gay American History, p. 647.

Chapter 2. The Boiling Point

30 "We're taking the place": Carter, *Stonewall*, p. 137.
30 "it became necessary to lay down roads": Ibid., p.
    9.
31 Mary Casal, *The Stone Wall: An Autobiography*:
    Reprint, New York: Arno Press, 1975.
32 A little after 1 A.M.: For more on the first night of
    the riots, see Tree interview; Storme DeLarvarie, a
    Stonewall-era veteran, interview by the author,
    May 10, 2006, Chelsea Hotel, New York City; Du-
    berman, *Stonewall*, pp. 181–212; Carter, *Stonewall*,
    pp. 129–82.
34 Storme DeLarverie: DeLarverie interview.
38 "They've lost that wounded look…": Allen Gins-
    berg, interview by Lucian Truscott, quoted in
    Carter, *Stonewall*, p. 199.
38 Tom Willenbecher, a historian: Tom Willenbecher,
    untitled essay, series 4, box 10, Rodwell Papers.
39 There are over 10,000 bodies: Christopher Street
    history based on Carter, *Stonewall*, pp. 6–11.
40 In 1962, eleven-year-old Ray Rivera: Rivera's his-
    tory draws on Andrew Matzner, "Rivera, Sylvia
    (1951–2002)," GLBTQ-The Encyclopedia of Gay,
    Lesbian, Bisexual, Transgendered, and Queer Cul-
    ture, online encyclopedia, http://www.glbtq.com/

social-sciences/rivera_s.html; "Profile of Sylvia";
Duberman, *Stonewall*, pp. 65–71.

40 The law was originally written: Carter, *Stonewall*,
p. 15.

Chapter 3. Organizing

46 "the homophile movement's first East Coast militant": Carter, *Stonewall*, p. 212.

46 "effeminate boys in the streets…": Ibid., p. 213

46 " Stonewall happened along…": Willenbecher, Rodwell Papers.

47 "Oh [it's] just a riot…": McGarry and Wasserman,
Becoming Visible, p. 22.

47 Shelley and a number of others: Martha Shelley's
story and the creation of GLF is pieced together
from profiles by Matt Koymasky and Andrej Koymasky at andrejkoymasky.com, and Paul D. Cain,
"Shelley, Martha," KeepMedia.com, an online encyclopedia of LGBT history in America; see also
Carter, *Stonewall*; Duberman, *Stonewall*; and Mc-
Garry and Wasserman, *Becoming Visible*.

48. "That's it! That's it!": Carter, *Stonewall*, p. 214.

48 "We are a revolutionary group…": See Carter,
Stonewall, p. 219.

48 "dismantling heterosexual marriage": Ibid.

49 Gay Activists Alliance: The history of GAA draws
on Marc Rubin, "GAA Must Be Restored to History," gaytoday.com/garchive/viewpoint/
083099vi.htm; see also Carter, *Stonewall*; Duberman, *Stonewall*; and McGarry and Wasserman,
Becoming Visible.

50 "There will be no heterosexual marriages to-day...": Rubin, "GAA Must Be Restored to History."

56 Lavender Menace: The history of Lavender Menace is based on information in GLBTQ.com; Carter, *Stonewall*, and Duberman, *Stonewall*.

60 On the morning of Sunday, June 28: Rodwell interview.

61 "The night of the Stonewall Riots...": Ibid.

62 "I was always so afraid...": Ibid.

62 Many in the New York chapter: McGarry and Wasserman, *Becoming Visible*, p. 151.

62 both groups changed their positions: Duberman, *Stonewall*, pp. 270–72.

63 June 22 through June 28, 1970: Craig Rodwell, letter announcing Christopher Street Liberation Day March, series 3, box 4, Rodwell Papers.

64 "more people would be free to participate...": Rodwell interview.

66 Welcome to the first anniversary: Craig Rodwell and Christopher Street Liberation Day Committee, flyer, Rodwell Papers.

68 "Aside from a few predictable...": Duberman, *Stonewall*, p. 280.

70 Parents and Friends of Lesbians and Gays: The organization's history is pieced together from Eric Marcus, "Morty Manford: Fearless Youth," http://www.gaytoday. badpuppy.com/garchive/people/100797pe.htm; Tom Owens, "One Mother's Voice: PFLAG Cofounder Recalls Groups Beginnings" and "History," www.pflag.org/history.

Chapter 4.
Our Sexual Revolution

81   Although gay men served as a tourist attraction: George Chauncey, *Gay New York* (New York: Basic Books, 1994), p. 167.

81   Many of those places: Wayne Hoffman, "The Great Gay Way," *Village Voice*, June 22, 2001.

83   In May of 2006: James Withers, "Preserving West Village Gay History," *Gay City News*, June 22–28, 2006.

84   By the mid-1950s, the shipping industry: The history of the piers' importance in the LGBT sexual revolution is based on Joseph Lovett, director, *Gay Sex in the 70s*, New York, 1974.

85   "Commercial trucks that hauled…": Carter, *Stonewall*, pp. 36–37.

86   "What made Christopher Street so gay…": Lovett, *Gay Sex in the 70s*.

87   "If we had our druthers": Carter, *Stonewall*, p. 36.

88   A drab and gritty working-class: Michael Shernoff, "Early Gay Activism in Chelsea: Building a Queer Neighborhood," *LGNY*, July 6, 1997.

89   "The Eagle, The Spike, The Ramp…": Ibid.

90   "trying to steal my soul just by looking at me…": Robert Guenther, "Remembering Jörg Wenz," *News from the Leather Archive and Museum*, Fall 2005.

90   "encourage cleanliness in the tenement districts": Chauncey, *Gay New York*, p. 208.

91   "baths visited by straight as well as…": Ibid., p. 209.

91   "The easiest and most comfortable place…": Lovett, *Gay Sex in the 70s*.

92 "the largest bathhouse in the country": As reported on gaytubs.com, a website dedicated to the history of New York City's gay bathhouses.

94 "I was so sex obsessed...": Edmund White, "The Continental Baths," gaytubs.com/More.htm.

Chapter 5.
The Response to AIDS

98 By the mid-1970s, huge advances: An interesting history of both the Chelsea Gay Organization and SMASH is provided by Shernoff, "Early Gay Activism in Chelsea.

100 "None of the political crazies...": Randy Shilts, *And the Band Played On* (New York: St. Martin's Press, 1988), p. 90.

100 Friedman-Kien spoke to the assembled men: Ibid., pp. 90–91.

102 On September 7, 1981: The history of the GMHC is based on Larry Kramer, *Reports from the Holocaust: The Making of an AIDS Activist* (New York: St. Martin's Press, 1994); Shilts, *And the Band Played On*; and Larry Kramer, untitled article, at amfar.org, "Public Service Announcement" link.

105 "A group of about fifty...": Kramer, *Reports from the Holocaust*, p. 51

106 "Paul Popham and I...": Ibid., pp. 22–23.

108 Kramer has said of his decision to write a play: Larry Kramer, comments at a press conference for the DVD release for the film *Women in Love*.

109 "AIDS...is the saddest thing...": Kramer, *Reports from the Holocaust*, p. 94.

110 On the morning of March 24, 1987: For the history of ACT UP see Kramer, *Reports from the Holocaust*; Shilts, *And the Band Played On;* ACT UP website, actupny.org.

113 "I had no idea what I wanted…": Kramer, *Reports from the Holocaust*, p. 137.

114 "On March 14, almost four years ago…": The speech is printed in its entirety in Kramer, *Reports from the Holocaust*, pp. 127–36.

118 ACT UP'S Achievements: These highlights are from the timeline on the organization's website, actupny.org.

Chapter 6. Pride

122 Heritage of Pride calls itself: The source of the history of the organization and its accomplishments is Phil Mannino, chairman of Heritage of Pride, interview by author, May 6, 2006, at Heritage of Pride office.

124 "HOP feels…": Ibid.

124 Organizers call it: From the Heritage of Pride website, hopinc.org/events/dance.cfm.

127 On the evening of April 24, 1993: The primary sources for the history of the Dyke March are Sara Pursley, "A Brief History of the Dyke March According to Me," *Gay City News*, June 7, 2006, and McGarry and Wasserman, *Becoming Visible*, pp. 250–51.

128 In their first action: McGarry and Wasserman, *Becoming Visible*, p. 251.